Wilderness Blessings

Wilderness Blessings

How Down Syndrome
Reconstructed Our
Life and Faith

Jeffrey M. Gallagher

CHALICE
PRESS

ST. LOUIS, MISSOURI

Cover image: DepositPhotos
Cover design: Scribe, Inc.
Interior design: Lynne Condellone

www.chalicepress.com

Print: 9780827243088   EPUB: 9780827243095   EPDF: 9780827243101

10   9   8   7   6   5   4   3   2   1   13   14   15   16   17

Cataloging in Publication Data from the Library of Congress available upon request.

Printed in the United States of America

for Kristen, Noah and Jacob
my three greatest blessings

CONTENTS

ACKNOWLEDGMENTS

I never started out to write a book. Honestly. I started out looking for a way to let our congregation know what was happening with the birth of our second child without having to answer emails and phone calls ad nauseum. We read about CarePages in a Boston Children's Hospital publication. We set up our page and invited people to come. And they did. Lots of them. Lots of you. Day after day I posted and you came and read and posted back. My writing became cathartic; the responses we received were therapeutic; and people kept telling me that I should turn this into a book—that this was a story that people would benefit from reading. I didn't know it then, but each comment was a seed that began to germinate in the wilderness of our lives—showing me that beauty and blessing could be found even in the darkest thicket of woods. Soon thereafter *Wilderness Blessings* was born. But it took an awful lot of people to get me from hasty bedside posts in the ICU to the germination of those seeds that follows.

I need to thank a lot of people.

Thank you to the members and friends of the congregation I am blessed to serve: the First Congregational Church of Kittery at Kittery Point, United Church of Christ. You were the ones who loved my family and me through this journey, who afforded me the sabbatical time to write this manuscript and process my journey even more thoroughly, and you were the ones who convinced me that this story needed to be told. I am truly and deeply blessed to serve such a caring and faithful congregation.

Thank you to the amazing crew at Boston Children's Hospital. The doctors, nurses, and staff, are far too numerous to name, but they are the ones who wrestled a blessing from the hands of tragedy by saving Jacob's life, more than once. What words can be said for such a gift except: thank you.

Thank you to my amazing family and friends who supported me, encouraged me, spread the word about *Wilderness Blessings* on social media, allowed me to talk about you in the pages that follow, listened to me talk about the project *all the time*, and were as excited as I was when this finally came to completion. You were the ones made it possible for us to survive what was the most challenging year of our lives. Your love, help, and support did not go unnoticed. We are deeply, deeply grateful and love you very much.

Thank you to Rev. Dr. Marvin Ellison for his wise counsel and open ear in helping me search for a suitable publisher for this work. Thank you to David C. McBride, Esq. for the generous gift of his time and legal assistance during the publication process.

Thank you to Brad Lyons, Publisher and President of Chalice Press, for always being quick to return email after email and for believing in this project, wholeheartedly, from day one. Thank you to Rebecca Woods for her keen editing eye in shaping the final version of this manuscript. Thank you to Gail Stobaugh, Amber Moore, Connie Wang, Lynne Condellone, and the rest of the amazing Chalice Press staff for allowing me to be an integral part of every decision needed to make *Wilderness Blessings* a reality. I couldn't have asked for a better team to work with.

Thank you to Rev. Dr. Jack Lynes for providing pastoral coverage at home when I needed to slip away to work on this project, and for his willingness to read through an early version of this work, and in his wise and honest way, for helping to make it so much better than I ever dreamed it could be.

Thank you to Rev. Dr. Elizabeth Hoffman for her fabulous foreword and for being my editor-in-chief, my sounding board, my conscience, my most honest critic, and my chief cheerleader. This project *would not* have happened without you behind me every step of the way. I am deeply grateful to you for your collegiality, wisdom, love, and friendship, and pray that this work might have earned me an honorary orange shirt. Thank you from the bottom of my heart.

Thank you to Kristen, Noah and Jacob. What can I say other than you three are the inspiration behind every single word in this book and every breath I take in life. Thank you for believing in me, loving me, supporting me, encouraging me, and helping to make me the person that I am today. You are my three greatest blessings in life, and I love you dearly.

And finally, thanks be to God, who has shown me that it is sometimes life's wilderness moments that provide the greatest blessings....

J.M. Gallagher

FOREWORD

by Rev. Dr. Beth Hoffman

There were never enough blankets. Lost within the overwhelming walls and wandering through the long desert halls of the Children's Hospital, it always seemed to me that there were never enough blankets for the patients or their families. Even when flushed with illness or feverish with hope, I was cold and always on the lookout for an extra set of covers for my hospital bed, my wheelchair or the operating table. And when my seven-year-old sister would come to the sixth floor to visit me, an extra blanket would be just the right thing for creating an oasis of protection, love, and imagination. We would hoist a fortress of covers and create a tented world where burned legs didn't need to be fixed, medicines weren't swallowed, I.V. tubing was filled with chocolate milkshakes, and bodies didn't hurt: a place where disability wasn't a disadvantage. But alas there were never enough blankets to sustain our desert mirage.

There was never quite enough material to create the superhero capes my little sister and I fashioned over and over again trying to make our family impervious to the bone break of the surgeries, or the heartbreak of having to live in the hospital, so young, for so long. In the wilderness of that high-tech hospital, I was always looking, searching, and reaching for a low-tech blanket that would give me a barrier of protection from the hurt, hide my shivering, disguise my trembling, and snuggle me tightly in the middle of the night, when all I knew for certain was that the nightlight by my bed was not enough to show me the way out of the dark.

Pushing the call button to bravely ask for more covers, I remember being able to pray eleven whole prayers before the nurse came. One prayer for every year I had been alive. When the nurse finally appeared, and asked what I needed, I couldn't really say I believed there would never be the right blanket, and I was left with my wild trembling;

alone, even as I knew my family was trembling in their beds at home. We all needed more cover.

When I pushed that call button over thirty years ago, wondered if the cord was hooked up to the nurses' station, or as I secretly hoped with my eleven prayers, to God's station, I didn't know that someday I would find the cover I was yearning for in the pages of this book. I thought there were never enough blankets and that we who needed cover would continue to shiver in the desert of disability.

Jeff Gallagher as father, pastor, and friend knows what it is to tremble in the wilderness. Refreshed by a wobbly faith, drinking the water from his own plentiful tears, and denying the temptation to turn back, he writes a reflective memoir that makes enough room in the tent for all, starting with his beloved son Jacob. *Wilderness Blessings* is a blanket of words that cools the frantic fever of human isolation and warms the soul with the honest struggle of expectations lost and then resurrected.

With stories of family, faith, and fear winding through the pages like gentle gauze bandages, Jeff offers no rescue for those, like himself, who are on a journey through this hard desert. Instead he kneels in triage mode, and offers his own aid kit to those who are wounded from daring to wrestle a blessing from the desert of disability. And as the bandages are gauze, each chapter is a thin place. Those who need tending can layer Jeff's stories and carefully realize that through them, they are seeing their own. Nothing is pulled too tight. No reflection is forced. No theology is aggressively tucked in. There is room for wounds to breathe, for spirits to heal, and for readers to accept the challenge to see the desert not as a barren wasteland but as a daring place of renewal.

Filled with deeply personal observations, desires, and confessions as both a child of God and as a parent of a child of God, Jeff leaves no desert stone unturned, no mirage intact. With an insider's eye that earns him an honorary lifetime membership in the world of disability, despite an able body, he writes of the horrors and the hopes of his child's hospitalization:

And so there's a camaraderie that develops, there's a kinship, there's a level of understanding, of familiarity with those who are other, or different. It makes Children's a model for what the world *could* be—God's kingdom on earth—a place where people actually "see" each other, respect each other for who they are, understand that everyone has their own story.

In all that I have ever seen Jeff preach or promise, there is a spirit of camaraderie with every word. The work of *Wilderness Blessings* is no exception.

As he walks with you through these pages, you will feel the company of a new yet familiar friend who never claims to have the answers but always honors and embraces the need to ask the questions. In a world where disability is, sadly, a handicap—and struggling faith can be sorely interpreted as a disability—the world needs these words. In one tough moment of wilderness, Jeff writes, "Suddenly I wasn't sure I could believe my own words," but I assure you, contained within this book are words you can believe in.

It has been a privilege to walk with Jeff on this journey of words and wonderings. It is a privilege surpassed only by the honor of walking beside his young son Jacob, who has just learned the art of mobility. Both of us having worn braces on our legs, I take personal joy in Jacob's determined strides. Jeff has taken not one step of this work for granted and it is sturdy art that will, just as leg braces would, steady you in the place you find yourself and move you gently forward.

I was indeed comforted all those years ago by the possibility of a low-tech blanket in a high-tech hospital. A blanket was a source of warmth that I could understand and work with. I could understand my need to be sheltered long before I could understand God as my sheltering source. It is a blessing that Jeff understands this as well. Bubbling under and through the sands of these sentences, like a thirst-quenching spring, is an earnest theology that you learn with your heart and not with your head. *Wilderness Blessings* is a welcome addition to the collection of books written about disability theology, but it does not belong only on an academic shelf. It belongs on your coffee table, your nightstand, the hospital waiting room, the pulpit, and definitely in your backpack, so that you might be ready for what desert journeys are yet ahead. And in the scorching moments of the unknown and the feverish tremble of hope against fear. Remember to reach for this book and dare to build a shelter of welcome for all in the wilderness, including you. The directions for good tent making are here in these pages. Wrap yourself up in them and remember, there are enough blankets if we share, as Jeff and Jacob have done with us. Go ahead and push the call button. It works in the wilderness.

PROLOGUE

Wandering beneath the fluorescent lights of Walmart, my wife, Kristen, and I—along with our sons Noah and Jacob—were peering at the displays while all those happy smiley faces were peering back at us. With Noah's hand in mine, and Jacob cradled in the seat of the cart, a shopper approached us to admire our newest addition. Smiling, she peered into the car seat, gasped audibly, and then rushed down the aisle without saying a word. We were left standing in a wilderness of silence.

Our newborn child didn't look like the Gerber baby she had expected, and she had no idea what to say about it.

Raising a child with Down syndrome, such encounters have become everyday normal for us. In time, we would learn to move past such reactions. But getting to that sanctuary of understanding was a journey. It would take a reconstruction of Jacob's heart, and mine. My faith, my relationships with others, my understanding of God, my vision for the future—everything would need to be radically reconstructed.

But when my eyes finally adjusted to my new surroundings—reminiscent of Dorothy opening the door from grainy black and white to Technicolor vibrancy in *The Wizard of Oz*—I couldn't begin to believe what I saw.

God's wilderness blessings were everywhere.

MARCH 7, 2008

Thanks for viewing our CarePage! We set this up before the baby was born as a way to keep you all informed as to what's going on with the birth and subsequent surgeries. Supposedly e-mails will be sent to you every time we update this page (that is, if you choose to have them sent to you—we believe you can check or uncheck that box when you sign in to CarePages). But you'll need to come to this site to read what's going on and to see all the wonderful baby pictures!

So, how did the ultrasound go?" I said into my cell phone, leaving my classmates behind in search of the silence afforded by the cold Bangor afternoon. Zipping up my coat and flipping up my collar against the biting February winds, I shoved my quickly numbing free hand into my jeans pocket, as I waited for my wife Kristen to answer my question.

"Well…." she said.

It may seem strange that I wasn't with Kristen for her ultrasound, but this was simply one of many for Kristen. Too many to count, in fact, going back to Easter Sunday two and a half years earlier—well before her current pregnancy—to when Kristen and I were preparing for our oldest son Noah to be born.

And really that is where our first CarePage post, and this story, has its genesis—not with Jacob's birth, but with Noah's—two and a half years before I received that phone call….

After leading the church I serve through the holy season of Lent—including an exhausting Holy Week—I was looking for some "down time" following the three worship services we held on Easter Sunday. The familiar ride down through the barren trees on Route 95 south to see our family nearly lulled me to sleep.

For a March day this one was unusually warm. There was no snow in Kristen's parents' backyard—and even more surprisingly, no mud—so my nieces Molly and Lexi were out looking for Easter eggs that had been hidden in plain sight. The adults were sipping coffee, enjoying the

1

unseasonably warm day, and hoping to procure a piece of candy or two from the kids' discoveries, when Kristen made a discovery of her own.

"I'm bleeding," she said with tears in her eyes.

"Ok," I replied, nervously wondering what was going on, as we headed down the hall to what used to be her bedroom growing up. Trying to sound confident, although I was far from it, I said: "It's probably nothing. I think I remember our doctor saying that some bleeding is normal. Is it a lot?"

"Yes," she replied. And unfortunately it was. Not only was it a lot, but it was bright red—a clear sign to anyone who knows anything about pregnancies (read: not me) that things were not right. So we quickly paged our doctor. After waiting for her to return the page, we were instructed to head back up to our hospital in Maine to be checked out. Hanging up the phone, we stared into each other's tear-filled eyes, looking for answers that neither of us had.

Without even stopping to say goodbye, we raced out the door and began the long—and largely silent—drive back up north to York, Maine. The hospital in York is small and intimate—one of the reasons we chose it. The nurses were waiting for us when we arrived. We were ushered in to one of the birthing rooms—a familiar one that I had visited parishioners from our church in before, and one that I imagined our children would be born in some day. Today, perhaps? But it was not to be.

The nurse instructed Kristen to get on the bed and hooked her up to a machine that measures the baby's heartbeat. Then we waited for the doctor to arrive. And we waited. After what seemed like hours and hours (but was probably only a half hour) of sitting there and staring at a machine that we knew nothing about, our doctor arrived. She checked Kristen out, and much to our surprise, told her that an ambulance ride further up route 95 north to Portland, Maine, was in order.

Obviously something was wrong. Our doctor admitted that York Hospital could not handle the potential problems that our baby was having, and neither could I.

Something was wrong with my child. *My* child. Tear-choked on the phone with Kristen's father, that's all I could say.

It was determined that Kristen had had a placenta abruption. This meant that the placenta had pulled away from the wall of her uterus. Fearing that the additional blood in her uterus might put her into premature labor (she was only thirty-two weeks along), Kristen was put on medicine to stop her contractions and given a shot of steroids to help boost the baby's lungs, just in case. Later I would joke that Noah—whose sex was still unknown at this point—was rendered ineligible to pitch for the Red Sox by virtue of this shot. But not just yet—jokes were the furthest thing from my mind.

With doctors in and out checking Kristen's progress, it was a long afternoon and evening. Not really understanding the dangers of having a premature child, part of me was hoping that the baby would be born that night. That would remove some of the tension, I thought, and it would be kind of cool to have our first child on Easter. But fortunately that wasn't to be. Instead we both spent a sleepless night in the hospital. No change of clothes, combined with the "mattress" the hospital gave me, added up to a sleepless twenty-four hours—this after what is, perhaps, the busiest day and busiest season of my year. Mercifully Kristen's mother arrived the next day—overnight bag in hand—to allow me to go home and get some sleep. Kristen would not be leaving so quickly.

Kristen spent a week in the hospital during which time the bleeding stopped. She was then released to come home for four weeks of bed rest. And wouldn't you know, at thirty-six weeks and one day—literally the morning after Kristen stopped taking the medicine to halt her contractions—she grabbed me and said those hair-raising words: "I think I'm in labor." And did I mention that it was on a Sunday morning…at 7:30 a.m.? This, just thirty short minutes before our church's 8 a.m. service was set to begin!

Mercifully by that time, a parishioner was sitting in his car in the parking lot reading his newspaper, waiting for our church's early service to begin. Playing the stereotypical part of the frantic father-to-be to perfection, I raced out to his car, told him that I'd be taking Kristen to the hospital and would be right back. Who else was going to lead worship, I thought to myself. I could come back and lead worship and then race back to the hospital to see how Kristen was doing. After all, we really didn't know if she was in "real" labor yet or not.

We hopped in our car, and the ten minute drive down the winding ocean-side road took…well…less than ten minutes. I saw Kristen into her room—where she was hooked up to that now-familiar heartbeat-measuring machine—and I raced back to the church. Upon arriving back at our little white New England church, I was met by a group of parishioners who had heard what was going on, and barred me from entering. So back to the hospital I went—again, in under ten minutes.

By this time the doctor had arrived. Being such a small hospital, York had limited personnel on staff on a Sunday morning, and they did not feel comfortable allowing Kristen to go into labor there. If she needed a C-section, they said it might take too long to get the necessary personnel in to operate on her. This could be very dangerous to both Kristen and the baby. Once again we were headed back to Portland.

As we sat together over the course of a very long afternoon, now staring at different hospital walls, a machine told us every time Kristen had a contraction. Each time the machine did its thing I would proudly announce, "Hey, you're having a contraction," to which Kristen would reply—employing a dry, if not annoyed, sense of humor—"Thanks," as if I was telling her something she didn't already know.

With each contraction the doctors and nurses told us that the baby's heart was being stressed very severely. Mine was too. This was most certainly the case when, unbeknown to us, the baby's heartbeat nearly stopped completely (creating no small amount of panic from the nurses and staff who raced in at breakneck speed in anticipation of an emergency C-section). Once the baby stabilized, it was decided that Kristen would have a scheduled C-section that night. The baby's heart was being taxed too much, and it was very possible that he or she wouldn't survive labor. Not understanding the complexity of the situation, I was simply excited that this would be the day we'd meet our new addition.

And so it was that Kristen was wheeled off into a labor and delivery room. I was given a hairnet, gloves, and hospital gown and told to get dressed and then wait to be called. So I did what I could do: I watched the Red Sox. As they were finishing up their game in Tampa I was ushered into a bright and sterile operating room. After being seated next to Kristen—and sneaking an antsy peek over the curtain to see my child half in and half out of my wife (think "Alien")—we met Noah Michael Gallagher for the first time. At four pounds, seven ounces, Noah entered the world as healthy as any parents could have hoped.

This is why they were watching Kristen so closely as we were preparing for our second child to be born. They were concerned that Kristen's high blood pressure might cause another placenta abruption. But when I raced outside on that cold afternoon, I soon realized that with that tentative, "Well…." Kristen was calling to tell me something much worse.

MARCH 11, 2008

Well...so much for March 20th! Kristen and I went in for an ultrasound on Monday, March 10th. It showed that the fluid surrounding the baby was low, so they decided to go ahead and deliver. So, last night Kristen gave birth to Jacob Ottley Gallagher. He is 4 pounds, 9 ounces and 17" long. Immediately after birth he was taken to the Neo-Natal ICU and remains in that at Children's Hospital. Here's what we know...

There is a major heart defect. This will require surgery. Right now they are going over the images from an echocardiogram they took. This will help to decide what will happen. The aorta is smaller than they thought. This might mean that surgery will happen sooner than they had anticipated. But again, we don't know until the results of the echocardiogram come in. Following that, he will be facing multiple surgeries to correct the heart problem. In addition to this they will also be testing for chromosomal deficiencies (i.e., Down syndrome, etc.). He has some of the signs that he may have such a deficiency, but not all of them. So we'll have to wait and see.

The good news is, he and Mom are doing great! His breathing is good, heart rate is good, and blood pressure is good. He had an uneventful night last night and hopefully will keep that up! He's in the Neo-Natal ICU at Children's and will be moving to the Cardiac ICU later today. From there we'll see how things go.

In the meantime... check out our pictures. He's a peanut, but very cute. And boy does he have a healthy set of lungs on him! We appreciate all of your love, prayers, and support and promise to keep you updated as best as we are able. (By the way, the photos from the delivery room may say March 11th, but he was born on March 10th—the date on the camera is just wrong!) Until next time...

The "routine" ultrasound Kristen had at York Hospital revealed that there were only three chambers in the baby's heart. At least the ultrasound technician could only *see* three chambers. But this wasn't to concern us, we were told. It was probably just the way the baby was positioned. York Hospital simply didn't have the technology to see as much as they wanted to, so we needed to schedule a Level 2 ultrasound in Portland—a place we were very familiar with by now—just to make sure everything was ok.

About a week later—as soon as they could squeeze us in—we headed north to a medical office just across the street from where Noah had been born. The air was heavy inside when we arrived, as we realized that all those who were gathered were not there for the joyous ultrasounds that so many couples eagerly await. These were families who had problems, concerns, or high-risk pregnancies. Smiles in the waiting room were hard to come by.

As we were called to follow the technician into a dark room for yet another ultrasound, Kristen and I both had a feeling that things were not good. The technician was very quiet as she looked and looked and looked at the baby's heart. She spent a long time going over and over the pictures, and by this time—having had so many ultrasounds—we knew what we were looking at. I kept whispering to myself, "Come on, there's got to be a fourth chamber there somewhere," but I never saw one. And, unfortunately, neither did the technician.

When she finished the exam we were told to wait for the doctor to come in. Before he walked through the door we could hear the doctor and the technician conferring, softly, in the hallway. He was as somber as she as he confirmed what Kristen and I both suspected: the baby had a heart defect. I grabbed Kristen's hand as the tears rolled down her face and welled up in my own eyes.

As the news hit I managed to ask a question. "Is this something that can be fixed with surgery?" I stammered out. The doctor answered in the affirmative, but could give us no details. We'd have to wait until we could schedule a consult with a surgeon—which turned out to be four days later. That's when the tears began to roll for me. We left the room together. I nervously paced up and down the hallway, while Kristen, quite composed at this point, made our appointment.

"This can't be happening." "They must be able to fix the baby." "It's got to be a mistake." Those were questions we wouldn't have answered for another four days. Four days. Four long, grueling, sleepless nights. Later I would begin to realize that this must be what it's like for all the parishioners I counsel who are waiting for diagnoses, waiting for cancer tests to come back, waiting to hear about abnormal mammograms. I always reassure those people that God is with them in their time of trial, that there is no place in this world that they can go to that God has not already been.

But this wasn't someone else, this was me. This was my child, my wife, my family. Suddenly I wasn't so sure that I could believe my own words.

The ride home was a familiar one—although instead of sharing bad news while driving north, this time I got to share it from the southbound side of routes 295 and 95. I called my mom. I called Kristen's mom, who by this point was shuddering every time I called her at work—because it was never with good news. Kristen tried to call her sister Traci. She managed to get out the word "hi," before tearfully handing the phone to me.

I said words like "major heart defect," "very serious," and "we just don't know what can be done." Because we didn't, and wouldn't, for four more days.

That Sunday I led worship. I remember standing up in front of a congregation that had heard bad pregnancy news from me before, but nothing like what was to come. Somehow I was composed enough to tell them that the baby had a major heart defect, and that we would be finding out more on Monday. It wasn't until the hugs started coming after worship that my tears began to flow. I was used to comforting members of the congregation when they received bad news. Now the roles were reversed. They were the ones saying to me, "We love you," and "We'll be praying for you." I, for one of the few times in my life, had nothing to say back.

This is a strange position to be in. Not just the having nothing to say part (though admittedly that is pretty strange). Pastors are taught in seminary that we're not supposed to let the congregation take care of us—we're the ones who are supposed to be taking care of our parishioners, they tell us. But in reality, those lines aren't so clearly drawn. The pastor of a church in a small community like the one I was serving becomes a part of the family. So there are times that the pastor needs to care for others, and there are times that the pastor needs to be cared for. This was one time when I could use all the hugs and prayers I could get. After all, I would often stand in the pulpit and say that we need to care for one another. How could I not allow the congregation to practice what I preached? And how could I not accept their care? It was exactly what I needed.

Mercifully a weekend of driving Thomas the Tank Engine incessantly around in circles with Noah helped to pass the time for us. As Monday arrived, things began to look up. Over the weekend I had been praying, a lot. This was something I was used to, but not for myself. I seldom pray for myself and even less frequently pray for something specific to happen. That's not what I believe prayer is about. I don't view God as some divine vending machine, which, if we say the right words and punch in the right numbers, will give us whatever we want. (Come on Kit Kat!) Rather, I believe that prayer is about asking for God's strength to get us through whatever may come our way; and so that's what I was praying for—God's strength.

When offering a wedding homily, I often say that God will not completely shield couples from life's storms, but will offer them a shoulder to cry on when those storms hit. In other words, I believe in a God who is profoundly affected by the trials and tribulations we struggle through on earth—a God who suffers with us. But just what does that mean?

Classical theological views of God speak of God as unchanged and unchanging, of a God incapable of feeling and emotion. This is not the God I believe in, nor the God I was praying to. For if suffering and pain exist in the world, and if God is not moved by the suffering of God's children, then God is apathetic. And apathy is completely incongruous with a God of love. As feminist theologian Elizabeth Johnson writes: "The idea that God might permit great suffering while at the same time remaining unaffected by the distress of beloved creatures is not seriously imaginable."[1]

Rather, what is imaginable is a God who became human in the form of Jesus Christ, so that God would know how to suffer *with* God's children. And this is the way I believe God exists in this world—with us and *within* us. For when Jesus' earthly body ceased to exist on this earth, he promised, in Acts 1:8, that the disciples, and by extension, all of God's children, would "receive power when the Holy Spirit has come upon [them]." We then see that the Spirit was granted to the disciples on Pentecost, the birthday of the church. The image of the Spirit resting on all those present at the feast in tongues of fire clearly shows that God desires to be in relationship with us.

Being with us, and within us, God is then, necessarily, affected by the sufferings that we go through. And so affected, God is moved with compassion, which literally means to suffer *with* someone. Again, Elizabeth Johnson's words are powerful: "the presence of divine compassion as companion to the pain transforms suffering, not mitigating its evil but bringing an inexplicable consolation and comfort...Knowing that we are not abandoned makes all the difference."[2]

I was praying for a really strong shoulder, and really big arms to reach out and hold me tight so that I would know, without a doubt, that in my time of suffering, I was not alone. I needed to know that God was there suffering with me. And that's precisely the feeling I received. It made all the difference in the world.

It also helped to hear that the baby's heart could be fixed. It would be a three-step process, we were told. The first surgery would require the artery heading to the lungs to be banded—so the lungs didn't receive too much oxygen. This would happen shortly after birth. The second would be step one in a two-step procedure that would basically bypass what the doctor called a malformed fourth heart chamber.

This was all good news—very good news. The baby's heart had a chance to be fixed—exactly what we were hoping to hear. And no one, at this point, had mentioned those two words that would change our lives forever: Down syndrome. Those words were nowhere on our radar screen (or ultrasound) and wouldn't be for some time.

MARCH 12, 2008

Good afternoon, everyone. It's 1:30 p.m. on Wednesday, now. Thank you so very much for all your prayers and well-wishes. It means the world to all of us.

The latest is that Jacob needs to go in for surgery tomorrow (Thursday). His aorta needs to be repaired. His body is moving blood, but it's working too hard having to do so. So that will be happening at some point tomorrow (we don't have a time yet). The good news is that the chief surgeon at Children's will be doing the surgery. Jacob's blood pressure has been a bit low (so they've given him medicine for that), but his oxygen saturation and heart rate are good. They are exploring a couple of options as to how they will repair the aorta, but haven't firmly decided on which one yet. He is resting in the Cardiac ICU.

Once that surgery is done, we're still looking at some others to repair his heart. Those are still yet to be decided, but will come later on down the road. We are hopeful that Jacob might be able to come home after he recovers from tomorrow's surgery, before he has to go back in for the next one.

The news is still out on chromosomal abnormalities. The more we hear them talking, the more we think that Down syndrome is a very real possibility, but they haven't confirmed that yet. To be quite honest, that's the least of our concerns. As long as we can get Jacob a healthy heart, nothing else matters too much.

Kristen, Noah, and I are managing. It's been a bumpy road, for sure, but we're doing ok. Reading all your notes on this page has been incredibly heartwarming, and so we thank you for that.

To our church family…I guess my paternity time started sooner than I had anticipated! Since I will be in Boston all week, Rev. Jack Lynes will be in the pulpit on Sunday and may also be for Easter (he and I will touch base at the end of this week about that). Any pastoral concerns you may have, please contact Sara or Jack, and they will work to handle them.

Finally, please look at our pictures! I will try and update the page with some more later today (I don't have my camera with me now). So please do check back. And also know that even though Jacob's first pictures say March 11th, he was born on March 10th (the date on our camera was off by a couple of hours).

Again, thank you so much for your love, prayers, and support. You're all in our thoughts, for sure, and we will make it through this with your support. Until next time...

It's true. Down syndrome was the least of our concerns, even after Jacob was born. But we're not there yet.

Back when we shared the news of the baby's heart problems with family and friends we were met with an overwhelming response: We should be headed to Boston Children's Hospital. It wasn't far away, after all. And yet, it all seemed so overwhelming. Who would we call to even get seen by someone at Children's? Where would the baby be born? Getting appointments at the busy Boston hospitals was a nightmare. Would Kristen deliver in Maine and then have the baby flown to Boston? How would she manage without the baby nearby? How would I manage racing back and forth from Boston to Maine? And plus, we had already set-up a delivery date at Maine Medical Center. We didn't want to cancel after all the work they had done for us.

And yet, people kept telling us to go to Boston—especially Noah's pediatrician.

Kristen, I should probably mention, has worked for many, many years at the office where Noah's pediatrician is. He wanted us in Boston, so he contacted someone he knew—with connections, of course—and got us all set up for a consultation and ultrasound at Boston Children's Hospital. She also guaranteed us that we could deliver the baby at Brigham and Women's Hospital. All the hard work was done for us, so we decided to check it out.

The night before our scheduled consultation we stayed in a hotel just north of Boston. We didn't want to be late for our early morning appointment, and we wanted to get a jump on the notoriously horrible commute. So after a restless night of sleep, we managed to beat the Boston rush and arrived at the hospital very early. The experience was light years from what we had had in Portland.

This isn't to say anything bad about the care we received at Maine Medical. It was just a *feeling*. It's kind of like the day I knew that I was called to serve the church I now serve. In the tradition of the United Church of Christ, ministers covenant independently with churches. We have no bishops or higher-ups placing us in one ministry setting or another. So searching for a church is basically like interviewing for a job, just with (hopefully!) a lot more God mixed in. Anyhow, on the day I was scheduled to have my first interview, I arrived at the church early. Stepping outside of the car, I knew that I was someplace special.

The church is a traditional, old-fashioned, white New England meetinghouse. In fact, built in 1730, the church is the oldest one in continuous use in the state of Maine. It is located on a sharp bend in the road, with an equally old cemetery across the street, and looks out over the Piscataqua River. But this vision of beauty isn't why I felt called there. It was a feeling of home. It was a feeling of comfort. It was a feeling like I had been to this place before, even though I never had. It was, dare I say, a call from God.

And while I wouldn't say that the feeling I had at Boston Children's Hospital was a "call," it was that same feeling of reassurance and home that I felt at the church. This, right from the moment we walked through the large revolving glass doors (lettered with the word "Welcome" in every conceivable language) and made our way up the colorful stairs, following the kid-friendly fish symbols to our destination. I remember whispering to Kristen that Noah would love the "game" of following those signs to wherever we needed to be.

The waiting room here was much different. The air wasn't as heavy. Instead the room exuded a sense of serenity and confidence. The ultrasound technician who did the exam was cheerful and pleasant—talking to us throughout the exam, even making a few jokes, and the doctor we met with was confident and reassuring.

They did not hide anything from us. The baby did have a major heart defect. This would require surgery following birth, but they were confident that the baby would survive birth without any major problems. Plus, they also suggested that there may be other surgical options on the table. The three-step fix was certainly a possibility, but they wouldn't close out other options, including a procedure that would go into the baby's heart and recreate the malformed chamber, giving the baby a heart that would resemble most of the typically developing population. The final decision would be made once they could get an echocardiogram after the baby was born.

It felt right. So we went with it. We didn't know it then, but it may have been a decision that would save our baby's life.

MARCH 13, 2008

I am thrilled to tell you all that Jacob has come through surgery with flying colors. His aorta was successfully repaired this morning. He remains in Cardiac ICU, and will be there for some time. He has a chest tube, breathing tube, and a bunch of other tubes. These will all be removed as time goes by. Once the breathing tube is removed (24 hours or longer) they will begin to see if Jacob can feed, gain weight, etc. This will go a long way toward letting us know when he can come home, etc. So we'll watch, wait, and see. But the good news is that he made it through this surgery—one major hurdle cleared.

The other good news we got is that it looks like his heart can be repaired. Jacob's problem has been a small right ventricle. Initially they were unsure whether this ventricle could be repaired or whether he would need what essentially amounts to bypass surgery. If his heart can be repaired (as the echocardiogram is suggesting now), then this has a couple of benefits. First, it will leave Jacob with a normal heart (good for the long run). Second, it will only take one surgery to fix (at roughly 2-3 months). This would be in lieu of bypass surgery, which would require 3 surgeries to fix. So if it can be repaired, and right now they are optimistic that it can be, that is good news indeed.

Many of you have asked about Kristen. She is doing well. She's sore and tired, but looking beautiful and getting stronger each day. She's made it over to see Jacob a few times and will be going over again soon. We're confident she'll be back on her feet in no time.

I have to say that I thought today might be a good day when I walked into the Cardiac ICU at 6:10 and was met, first, by a chaplain. We prayed with Jacob, and it certainly set the tone for what has been a very positive day.

I also have to say that it is amazing how much love is coming through this website. Your notes have both buoyed our spirits and brought us to tears. Words cannot express how grateful we are to each and every one of you for your support.

So please continue to keep us all in your prayers. Jacob cleared one hurdle today, but he's got some more ahead. (And test results on the chromosomal abnormalities are still not available.) So as you keep us in your prayers, please add a prayer or two for the incredible staff, doctors, and nurses who work here at Children's. If you've ever doubted that miracles exist, just walk around this place for an hour or two—I have no doubt that you'll change your mind.

More updates and pictures soon. Until next time...

Much like Noah's birthday, we were not prepared for Jacob's. You'd think we would have learned by this point. Early on the morning of March 10, Kristen and I drove in to Brigham and Women's Hospital for our first meeting with the obstetrician. This was an adventure. Gone were the personal attentions lavished upon us by the staff at York Hospital. We were simply one of many waiting to see our doctor.

So after filling out the appropriate paper work and getting the obligatory "blue card"—your keys to the kingdom in the Boston hospitals—we finally met with the obstetrician. A few tests determined that the amniotic fluid surrounding the baby was low. At thirty-six weeks gestation, this was not something the obstetrician was comfortable with. And so, after leaving the room for a moment, she returned to surprise us with the question. "So, would you like to have a baby today?" Nine words I was not expecting to hear.

But not Kristen. Unbeknown to me she had actually packed a bag (just in case, she said), even though we were simply headed in for a routine appointment. Obviously that was not the case. After answering question after question about our family history and the pregnancy, and after Kristen being pulled aside by a nurse who felt compelled to ask if I was a danger to her or the baby (another sign that we were not in York anymore!), we were taken upstairs to be admitted to have the baby. This was the beginning of a very long day.

You see, while eating breakfast is normally a good thing, when you're about to have a C-section baby it's not looked upon so favorably. Before we could do anything, we had to wait for Kristen's food to digest. This meant we would deliver the baby in the early afternoon. But the nurse kept coming in to tell us that another "emergency" C-section had bumped us from our spot. And so we got to wait a little longer.

Trying to be a good husband, I vowed not to eat while Kristen was fasting in preparation for her surgery. I didn't think this would be too hard, given that the baby was supposed to be born in the early afternoon. But as the early afternoon turned into late afternoon and then evening and then late evening, my plan was coming unraveled. I was nervous, anxious, and starving, causing our nurse to keep trying to force-feed me saltines, determined not to have two patients in the delivery room!

This was, of course, after she had come into the room to have a "heart-to-heart" with Kristen. Since Kristen was just thirty-one years old, the nurse was questioning Kristen's decision to have her tubes tied following the C-section. Did we know that our baby might not be all right? Were we sure that we wouldn't want to try again if things didn't go the way we hoped? I deflected all questions to Kristen, who said, simply: "Have you seen my OB history? I'm done." The nurse looked over at me. I smiled. No other words needed to be said.

In retrospect this should have been another clue about the seriousness of the journey we were about to embark upon, but in the midst of the increasingly darkening wilderness, those sign posts are anything but easy to see.

Finally, after repeated phone calls to our families ("Did you have the baby yet?" "Sorry, no") we were brought to the delivery room. Actually, Kristen was. I, in my hairnet and blue scrubs (the Boston blue not that much different than Maine), was ushered to a chair in the middle of a hallway. This was a surreal experience. It must be that this is "the" partner's chair at Brigham and Women's. Just outside a pair of double doors heading into the operating areas, this single chair sits, lonely, against a plain white wall. No pictures to look at. No magazines to read. Just the person waiting to accompany the mother-to-be, alone with his or her thoughts. As people passed by, there were nods of acknowledgment. As if to say, "Good luck," "My prayers are with you," and "I hope all goes well." I imagine those who travel that hallway regularly have seen some pretty amusing sights there, with a wide array of nervous companions waiting to be called in, I among them.

Finally I was called in. Unlike Kristen's first C-section, this time I was nervous. Ok, having been through this before, and understanding that this was far from an ordinary birth, I was downright scared. The room was full of people—twenty, I would say, at least—with doctors, nurses, and interns galore, all there to make sure our new addition made a safe entry into the world. As Kristen and I sat behind the curtain—there would be no peeking this time around—we made some small talk, and we waited for our baby to be born.

It was sometime after 10 p.m. that Jacob Ottley Gallagher, weighing in at four pounds nine ounces (bigger than his brother), made it into the world. Immediately after breathing his first breath of sterile hospital air, Jacob was whisked away to an examination table, where a team of doctors and nurses made sure he was all right. All the while we were oblivious to whether we had a Jacob or an Emma! It wasn't until our baby was probably two minutes old that our nurse thought to come over and ask, "Did anyone tell you what you had? You had a boy!" Noah now had a little brother, and we had a second son. Tears of joyful apprehension flowed.

Once it was determined that Jacob was in no immediate danger, the room quickly cleared out. So quickly that Kristen, feeling every bit the afterthought, was left behind in virtual obscurity to be sewn shut. I followed Jacob to what I call a "holding room"—a place to reassess his condition, again, as we awaited the paperwork to send Jacob to the adjoining Boston Children's Hospital. In this room, as the clock ebbed closer and closer to midnight, I was exhaustingly overwhelmed. A doctor was carefully looking over Jacob. Two other babies were beside him. There were no balloons, no teddy bears, no joyful proclamations that new lives had been born. Just the stark realization that these babies needed some serious attention.

Weak-in-the-knees, sweating, and feeling as though I was in a tunnel that was closing fast, I came close to passing out, but managed to accompany Jacob on his ride across the bridge to Children's. Because there was no room for him in the Cardiac ICU, he was brought to the regular Neo-Natal ICU (NICU). He would rest there until morning, when they would do a very thorough echocardiogram to see what they had to work with. I was off to find Kristen (no small task in the maze of hospitals) in the hopes of getting some sleep. And sleep I did. The stress of the day finally caught up to me, and I managed a few hours, before heading back over to the NICU to see what lay in store for our brand new baby boy.

Remember I mentioned miracles in the CarePage update? We'll have to wait a bit on that. As is the case, so often in life, when things are hectic, when life is throwing things at us faster than we can handle, we don't notice the ways in which God is moving in our midst. That was certainly the case on the day Jacob was born. God was working, but the wilderness was too overwhelming to see where or notice how. It wouldn't be for another few days that I would begin to see just how active God had been—a pattern that we have been blessed to be in since Jacob breathed his first breath.

MARCH 14, 2008

Once again, thank you so much for all the love, prayers, and support you are sending. We may be here in Boston—away from many of you—but the sentiment comes through loud and clear. It really has been one of the big reasons why we've made it through these last few days.

Today we'll start with Kristen. She was discharged from the hospital this morning. She walked all the way from Brigham & Women's to Children's Hospital (which is quite a walk, even though they are connected). She's doing very well. In fact, you wouldn't even know she had surgery, she's doing so well!

Jacob had a great night. His vitals continue to be good. They removed his chest tube this morning (earlier than we had thought). The next step will be to remove his breathing tube. He has been breathing on his own, mostly, so they are thinking that they'll give that a shot this afternoon. Once we make sure that goes well, the next step will be to see about getting him some food. One step at a time, but they all continue to be forward steps—and for that we're grateful.

Jacob still remains in Cardiac ICU and will for the foreseeable future. Noah is doing great at home with his grandparents, aunt and cousins. He saw some pictures of Jacob last night and immediately referred to him as "my Jacob." Good news indeed!

That's all for now. Jacob is resting well and we'll be in to see him again in a couple of minutes (no computers allowed in the ICU). Check out the photos. We've added a few new ones for you.

Thanks again, for your amazing support. We can't wait to see you all and to let you all hold Jacob for yourselves! Until next time...

Very early on the morning after Jacob was born, the cardiologists did a long echocardiogram (ECHO) to see exactly what was going on with Jacob's heart. They could tell a bit of what was going on before he was born, but this ECHO would give them the definitive pictures as to what they were looking for. After the large machine had been wheeled away from Jacob's bedside in the NICU, we were given a chance to hear what they had found.

The good news: Jacob's heart was no worse off than they had thought. The ECHO confirmed that Jacob was operating with about three and a fourth chambers. There were valves where there shouldn't have been, and no valves where they should have been. In the miraculous way in which the body adapts, Jacob's body had somehow managed to figure out a way to keep things working, even with his badly malformed heart. But it was no worse than they had anticipated. Actually, it might have been even a bit better. Our cardiologist suggested that the malformed chamber could possibly be salvaged. This would mean one surgery instead of the three-step repair. But the final determination wouldn't come for a while. They needed to watch Jacob grow, see how his heart reacted, and wait before deciding definitively. That was the good news.

The bad news was that the ECHO showed that Jacob's aortic arch was significantly narrowed—too narrow for blood to flow through. Because this sometimes shows up in children born with heart problems, Jacob had been put on some medicine to keep a duct open that would allow blood to flow through—but he couldn't stay on this forever. Jacob would need to have his aortic arch repaired, in just two days. This meant that our newborn child would be heading in for major heart surgery at less than three days old.

Thinking that we knew what the wilderness was like, we were quickly learning how dark that forest of trees could get.

Over the course of the next day and a half, Jacob was moved out of the NICU and placed in the Cardiac ICU. This is where they wanted him all along. I shuttled Kristen back and forth, more often than not in a wheelchair, so she could see her new baby boy. But we couldn't hold him. Jacob was attached to so many tubes and had so many lines coming out of him, that we had to be entirely hands off. We could walk up to the side of his crib, touch his hands and face, kiss him on the cheek, but holding wasn't an option. It was a sad but necessary reality that we would come to know all too well during our hospital stays.

When the day for surgery finally arrived, I was asked to arrive at the hospital very early—around 6 a.m. I was told to head straight to the cardiac ICU, to sign some paperwork and send Jacob on his way. It was there, to my surprise, amid all the presurgery formalities, that I was granted an amazing and unexpected gift: the opportunity to hold my son for the first time.

While I wasn't able to put any perspective on it then—the emotion of it all was just too raw—a few months after that morning, on Christmas Eve, actually, I found myself sharing my experience with the congregation. It was the first time I had ever shared that experience with anyone, and so I'll let those words speak for themselves:

> *While preparing for our Christmas worship services, I found myself listening to a bunch of different Christmas CDs to get myself in the Christmas spirit. (As if the snow wasn't enough, I know!) Anyway, one of the CDs I kept turning back to was "The Christmas Sessions" from the contemporary Christian rock band MercyMe. While I am not a huge fan of contemporary Christian rock music, I was struck by this CD, mainly because of the one original track MercyMe has on the album, entitled: "Joseph's Lullaby."*
>
> *And so to start tonight, I'd like to play this song for you. It is sung from Joseph's perspective, as a heartfelt prayer of hope that before Jesus becomes who he is destined to be, Joseph might experience the overwhelming joy of knowing Jesus simply as his newborn child. [Here I played the song]:*
>
> *And I continued…Although I had heard this song before, it struck me particularly poignantly when I heard it again just over a week ago; and if you'll indulge me to tell some tales from my own life, I'll explain why. Most all of you know that this has been a trying year for my family. Back in March our second son Jacob was born, and although he is doing well now, Jacob's journey has not been an easy one. He has had two heart surgeries already, and has spent nearly two of his nine months in the hospital.*
>
> *Well, the first of those two surgeries happened when Jacob was just two days old. On the morning of that surgery I can remember going into the hospital very, very early—well before dawn. Kristen was still at Brigham and Women's Hospital, having just given birth, of course, and so I went to the Cardiac ICU to see Jacob to surgery by myself. After being greeted by—and saying a prayer with—one of the hospital chaplains, the nurse caring for Jacob was nice enough to unhook him from all the lines he had attached to him, so that I could hold him before sending him off. And then he stepped out of the room.*
>
> *I can remember the scene now as vividly as if it was yesterday. The room was dark, save for the subtle lights coming from a couple*

of monitors in standby mode. It was quiet—much quieter than the normal ICU, because there were no alarms going off. And it was early in the morning, so there was little commotion in the hallway. It was just me, in the dark quiet of that hospital room, holding my brand new son—asleep in my arms—completely oblivious about what was to happen.

And I can remember feeling exactly the way Joseph did in that song: hoping that before all of the surgeries and heartache and trying times to come, we might enjoy a peaceful and joy-filled moment as father and son. And that's exactly what we received. It was a moment I never wanted to end. While I would hardly classify myself as Joseph—nor would I label Jacob as Jesus—I did have that very profound desire to hope and pray that the dreams for my slumbering child might be fulfilled. As Joseph sings in that song, I knew that Jacob had no idea what was in store for him, and so I was hoping and praying that for just one moment he might know God's peace and comfort before setting off on his very difficult course before him.

For we knew the road before him was going to be tough—not that we knew then how tough it was going to be—but the Dad in me was just hoping Jacob might know some peace, even if it was just for that moment. It was a profound moment for me, and one that I haven't shared with anyone until now.

And such, it wasn't until I heard "Joseph's Lullaby" again this year, that I made these connections, and began to realize that—in a very real way—that, this year, I have a completely new perspective on what Christmas is all about. For I admit that up until now I have always been focused on what it is that we have received on this most blessed night.

And that's not a bad thing, because we have received quite a gift, for sure. For on this night we were given the gift of Jesus, the one who would grow up to be the Christ, and live a life that would teach all of us what it means to be truly loving, and of the potential that humanity has to live in peace and harmony with each other. That's the gift we received on this night, in that Bethlehem stable, so long ago.

But this year I'm realizing that this is just one way to look at Christmas. For while we may want to focus on the receiving end, there is also the giving end. Now I don't mean presents and all of that; but rather, I think that part of Christmas is paying some attention to who gave this gift and what it is that they felt that they were giving us.

For I have to say that once I walked Jacob down that long hallway and gave him a kiss before watching him get wheeled through those operating room doors, I began to understand what it was that Joseph, Mary, and God gave to humanity on that very first Christmas. And that was: the gift of faith, hope, and trust.

For if you have ever had to take a loved one—someone you care about very deeply—and release them into the care of someone else, knowing that their life depended on how that person acted, then you can begin to know what it was like to give this Christmas gift. For is that not what God, Mary, and Joseph did? In bringing Jesus into the world—and then releasing him to do the work he did—they basically said to humanity, "We are putting all of our faith, hope, and trust in you—please get it right, for the sake of our son."

And while I think we would have to admit that we haven't gotten it right yet, completely—for the world still does not know the peace that Jesus came to show us—the amazing thing is that every year, every year, we get a chance to try all over again. For on this night it is as if God wipes the slate clean again. It's as if God says, "I've done it once, I've done it 2,000 times, I'll do it again—here's Jesus, my faith, hope, and trust are in you to get it right."

Given this, I wonder what it would be like if we shifted our perspective just a bit this year? Instead of focusing on what we have received, what if we focus on the givers and what they gave? Would that new perspective shift the way we live in response to what happened in that stable some 2,000 years ago? I don't know, but I believe that the world would surely benefit if a few of us gave it a try.

And so that is my hope and prayer for you, my friends, this year—to view Christmas, the birth in the stable, and the baby through the eyes of those from whom this gift has been given to us all. God, Mary, and Joseph put their trust in us to receive their son and get it right. And since there is no peace on earth just yet, it seems that we have some work to do.

But you can save that work for tomorrow—there will be time enough to get started. For tonight, just enjoy the newborn baby, imagine the dark stable with all its sights and sounds, dream with Mary about what the child may become, and go out with the words of that lullaby on your lips. Amen.

And Amen.

MARCH 15, 2008

Again, thank you so much for all your thoughts and prayers.
They are what is keeping us going through this trying time. This
webpage has been a tremendous gift to us. Thank you all for being
a part of it.

Not a lot of new news today. Jacob will have his breathing tube
removed this afternoon. Right now he's getting some steroids to
boost his lungs (this also means he won't be pitching for the Red Sox
anytime soon!). Once they pull that tube, we will start working on
feeding. We should also get a lot more access to him at that point
and be able to hold him. We also heard today, for the first time, that
if all goes well, he might be moved out of ICU to the inpatient rooms
in the next day or two. Just some more positive steps, which we like.

Kristen is feeling good. She got a good night's sleep at her
parent's house last night. I got to go running in the rain and snow
this morning—which is always a good thing.

We'll post more pictures once we get that breathing tube out
of him. And hopefully there might be a few with Kristen and me
holding him—we'll keep our fingers crossed.

That's all for now. Until next time…

The day of surgery. You know that Jacob came through the surgery
fine—as the CarePages have revealed as much—but that's not to
say that Mom and Dad fared as well. In the months and years to come
after Jacob's surgeries I would often say that Jacob had the physical
scars, but Kristen and I had the emotional ones. This was definitely a
day of scarring.

With Kristen still back at Brigham and Women's at this point, my
task was, literally, to race back and forth between the two hospitals
getting and giving updates. It's a good thing, actually, because I
couldn't have taken sitting in that waiting room all by myself. It's a
nerve-wracking place to be. Children's does as much as they possibly

can to make it a good experience. They have incredibly patient and understanding staff members who function as liaisons between the operating and the waiting room (a nurse in the operating room calls out at periodic intervals...the chest tube is in, the baby is on the heart machine, surgery is finished, etc.). But let's face it, how good can things be when your child is in for surgery? One woman let the staff working in the waiting room know this in no uncertain terms.

In actions that can only be described as hysterical, this parent bellowed, cried, and hollered for updates on her child when they weren't coming in fast enough. If she was looking for sympathy from the rest of us, she was in the wrong place. She talked (sorry, YELLED) on the cell phone to whomever she could get in touch with. This drama went on for the entire time that I was able to stay within those four walls.

Now, normally I'm not one to comment on anyone else's experience in life. After all, we don't know what it's like to walk in another's shoes. My son was having major heart surgery so I could relate...But not really. You see, this woman's daughter was simply having her tonsils out. Now granted, there should probably be no such use of the word "simply" when we're talking about surgery, but really? A tonsillectomy? I had all I could do not to stand up and yell at her in my best Boston-accented, rush hour traffic voice (one that I confess I use more than I should) that I knew what she could do with her cell phone! But I didn't. I bit on my hand and chose that moment to head back down to the Children's Hospital lobby.

It was there—thanks be to God—that I happed upon another family in our church whose daughter had come in for an appointment. This family was a much-needed diversion. Not only do the mother and I share a passion for running (a passion which will figure prominently into the story in just a bit), but being able to assume the role of pastor and care for a parishioner—as I checked in to see how she and her family were doing—was just what I needed. In fact, I talked for so long, that I completely lost track of time until my cell phone rang, and I was told to come back up and get the word on Jacob. A good thing, for many reasons—not the least of which was the fact that I wouldn't need to go back in that waiting room and see that hysterical mother again.

I know, this hardly sounds like the voice of a pastor who had just finished offering pastoral care, but as I walked back to that waiting room I was just a Dad—a Dad who, in that moment, cared more for his family than anyone else on earth; and a Dad who just happened to have a few new teeth marks on the back of his right hand.

MARCH 16, 2008

Another day and another few steps forward. The breathing tube came out, but a feeding tube went in (it's hard for Jacob to figure out how to eat from a bottle until he figures out how to digest food). We started with some Pedialite and then advanced to some formula—that went quite well. The amount of formula will be increased throughout the night. Jacob still has some oxygen on, but it's at a very low level, just to give him a little hand. From here we'll see how things go. If he continues to tolerate food, and can reach a couple more milestones, he might just be able to move out of the ICU in the next day or so. So things are definitely progressing in the right direction!

We've posted a few photos new for you to look at (one of which might give you a hint what baseball team the little guy is going to support). Today was a busy day with lots of family in to visit, which was great, and Jacob was awake for a good portion of it! He especially seemed pleased when big brother Noah was looking over the bedside at him.

That's all for now. We'll hope for some continued progress tomorrow. Thanks, once again, for all your prayers, love, and support. Until next time…

A dad who cares more for his family than anyone else on earth. Yup, that about sums it up. That's why it felt so good to have so much of our family come in to visit Jacob in the ICU. Now this is hardly an easy prospect for members of the family. Our parents had been in a few times to see Jacob, but our siblings hadn't been. So although we were used to the tubes, the beeping, and the buzzing that accompanies a stay in the ICU, not everyone else was.

Yet that's what life is like for the family of a baby who isn't "perfect." (More on this label later, but for now we'll go with it.) What still amazes me as I rejoice over the birth of friends' babies, and as I celebrate in church the births in the lives of the families in our congregation, is how often things go flawlessly. Think about it. Think about all of those births that you have waited anxiously for in your life. The fact that you're reading this book might suggest that you are one of those for whom a birth didn't go perfectly, but even so, that's the way things go, more often than not.

"Mom and baby are doing fine," is a standard phrase I hear during the prayer time at church. This is not only a wonderful blessing for the family, but also—I say selfishly—a wonderful blessing for me, too—because then I can go and visit the baby knowing that the visit will be filled with joy and happiness (with my only concern coming from whether I'm going to drop in on an unsuspecting mother breastfeeding her newborn, thinking that I'm a doctor, as my face turns brighter than their newborn's cheeks). Mercifully this hasn't happened…yet…Hold on, I need to find a piece of wood to knock on….

Anyway, that's how new baby visits are supposed to go. I only know because I've been to them; I've never actually had people come to see my family at one. With Jacob (and Noah), our family and friends were forced to come in for those "other" visits. And we are blessed because they did it with ease. At least that's how they looked to me. But on the inside I'm sure they were struggling, as I know I would be.

Honestly, For I don't really remember a single word they said. All I know is that they showed up to be there, in our joyous grief, grief-tainted joy, or whatever kind of emotion it is that there's no properly worded greeting card for. (Incidentally, this is the biblical book of Job in a nutshell. When Job has all of that misfortune befall him in his life—dead children and cattle and physical sores, oh my!—you know what his friends do? They just show up. They show up and for seven days and seven nights they just sit with him. They don't say anything; they don't try to fix anything; they don't accuse him of anything; they just sit with him. It's when they open their mouths and start wondering what Job did to cause God to rain down misfortune on him that causes all hell to break loose.)

So my family and friends—whether they knew it or not—did the best Eliphaz, Bildad, and Zophar imitations that they could (minus the sack cloth and ashes, of course): they simply showed up. My friends and colleagues, Beth and Brad, came and visited Jacob and me (Kristen was still at Brigham and Women's) while he was in the NICU. They didn't pray eloquent prayers; they didn't try to make things right; they just came. They told me what a joy it was to see my new son, and that's just what I needed to hear. Knowing that they had given up hours of their overscheduled day to come and see us meant more than words could say.

25

And our family did the same. They showed up in the ICU and celebrated the new life in our family. Some of Jacob's cousins—Meghan, Patrick, Ryan, and Brendan—came with handmade cards that combined "Welcome to the family" and "Get well soon" in a way that the greeting card companies should take notice of. They were perfect. And they gave us all great comfort as we read them in the hours when there was no one to keep us company save for the beeping monitors and exhaling breathing machines.

And that's just it. When you're coming to visit a baby who's not "perfect," just show up. Don't be afraid. Don't stay away. Don't come in as if you're walking into the funeral home for visiting hours. Because you know what? A baby has been born. And whether that baby is on the earth for a few minutes, a few days, or 100 years, there's still much that needs to be celebrated. So perhaps you leave the six-foot plush Barney at home (actually a good idea regardless of the circumstances of birth), but just come. Come and be open to whatever the emotions are of those you have gone to visit. It's likely that they'll be looking to celebrate that their nine months of waiting and planning have come to an end—just like any other new parents.

And if, perchance, they need to cry, just do your best impersonation of God (by offering a shoulder to cry on, that is) and go with it. You can handle that too.

Interestingly, it may also be—in the days and weeks to follow—that people still will not know how to act around you if yours isn't one of those perfect births. What do they do? What do they say? Helpfully, another colleague brought this up a few weeks after Jacob was born. Wanting—no, needing—to celebrate the birth of her first grandchild, she didn't know how to do that in front of me. Could she really celebrate a perfect birth in front of someone for whom things were still touch and go? I was relieved to hear her voice those words, and I quickly assured her that I would be hurt if she *didn't* celebrate the baby. After all, a new life had come into this world, and regardless of the circumstances surrounding the baby's birth, that was plenty of reason to give thanks to God.

Which leads me to my favorite reaction—the best, by far, that I received from anyone after Jacob was born and diagnosed with Down syndrome (I know we're not there yet, but go with me). While sitting in the traffic just outside of Mecca (aka Fenway Park), I was on the phone with my good friend and colleague Beth. When I told her that Jacob had Down syndrome, her response was: "Congratulations! I sometimes think that people with Down syndrome are the way God intended for all of us to be, and the rest of us are just trying to figure that out."

Her words brought a smile to my face then, and they bring a smile to my face now as I write this. "Congratulations, you've just had a very special baby." Those are the words that *any* new parent needs to hear.

MARCH 17, 2008

Sorry for the late update, but it was a busy St. Patrick's Day. Jacob has moved out of the ICU! Yeah! Must be the luck of the Irish baby, huh? He is now in the cardiac inpatient ward and doing exceptionally well. He's being fed through a feeding tube in his nose, and happy as a clam (because he's got a full belly 24/7).

From here, feeding is the big issue. Tomorrow Jacob will start getting food for an hour, and nothing for two hours (to mimic what he would be getting normally). If all goes well there, he'll begin to start trying to feed with a bottle soon thereafter. From there we'll see how it goes. The better he does feeding, the faster he'll be coming home. One nurse suggested that he might just make it home for Easter. While that would be great, we're trying not to get our hopes up too high, lest we get disappointed. But it sure would be great to have him home for Easter. We'll just have to see.

You'll see in some of the pictures we've added that his aunt bought him a bunny hat. It kind of reminds me of Ralphie's costume in "A Christmas Story" (you know, the pink bunny suit), and I'm sure we'll hear about it when Jacob is older and able to be embarrassed by the pictures!

Just a note to my church family… I'm so glad that Jack led you through a meaningful Palm Sunday service yesterday. After much thinking, praying, and talking with Kristen, I have decided that I need to take this week off as well. Even though it is Holy Week—and it pains me not to be with you—I need to be here with Kristen, Noah, and Jacob. I trust you all understand. It is my hope to be back with you just as soon as things settle down, but it's just too early to say when that will be.

I say it every time, but we do, greatly, appreciate your love, prayers, and support. We can feel it all the way down here in Boston, believe it or not, and on this St. Patrick's Day, we feel pretty darn lucky to have you all in our corner. Until next time…

I remember the first night that Kristen and I took Noah home from the hospital, thinking to myself: "Are they really going to let us take care of this baby on our own? Where's the manual? Where are the classes we need?" Actually, there were classes. We were in them. We were in birthing classes at York Hospital; ironically we missed the last class on nontraditional births. Now I'm not talking water births or anything like that—I'm talking about those situations when things are less than perfect: emergencies, high-risk pregnancies, and the like. Yeah, that's the class we missed. The irony is certainly not lost on me! Perhaps York Hospital ought to think about offering that class earlier in the program. I guess they just don't want to scare people on day one, but it might be helpful. Anyway....

So moving from ICU to a regular room is kind of like taking your baby home for the first time. In the Cardiac ICU Jacob had either one-on-one or one-on-two care. This meant that, at most, one nurse was covering two children. There always seemed to be a nurse plainly in sight, so anytime we had a question, an answer was soon to be found.

Not so much on the regular floor. Now this is not a criticism of the hospital, it's just that the care is not—and needs not be—quite as intense. A warning for the parents might have been helpful, though, because I was muttering criticisms left and right. For we could now go for a half hour, or even an hour or more without seeing a nurse come by. This was positively absurd! My baby could be dying and they were out lounging at the nurse's station. Of course, this wasn't the case. But when you go from constant care to something else, it all of the sudden feels like you are very much on your own and have no idea what you're doing. And it's not a good feeling.

My reassurance, however, came from an unlikely place. Our roommates (you're also not alone when you leave ICU) were from Argentina. They spoke very, very little English, so we mostly exchanged smiles and glances back and forth across our cribs. Through overhearing the translators, we came to learn that they had chosen Children's Hospital because it was one of the best hospitals in the *world*. That's right, in the *world*. We were blessed that it was just over an hour down the road.

Our roommates had left Argentina a full four weeks before their baby was born to be sure that they would be in the United States when the baby arrived. Good plan, right? Too bad he chose to begin arriving while they were still en route and in the air. Mercifully the baby didn't arrive over the Atlantic, but in Boston when they got the mother on solid ground. The baby had a rare lung condition that was going to require a full lung transplant. So after having some surgery, they were waiting—thousands of miles away from home, in a country that was not their own and that didn't speak their language particularly well. And yet they were confident—you could see it in their faces and hear it in the prayers they prayed with the Catholic chaplain—that things were going to go well. It was enough to buoy my confidence as well.

We left before that family did, so I don't honestly know what became of their son. Just like I don't know what became of the young girl whose parents we saw going in and out of the Cardiac ICU for weeks (though they had been there for months) as she awaited a new heart. Just like I don't know what happened to all the families for whom those heart-stopping Code Blues were called.

But, despite my initial worries walking out of ICU, that family from Argentina gave me confidence that, odds are, things had a pretty good chance of turning out well.

Nevertheless it was heart wrenching to look at our young roommate. Big, thick staples ran right down the center of his chest, and it was clear that moving was a challenge for him. My heart ached every time I saw him. But in a place like Children's Hospital such sights are the norm. Walk down the hallway and see the young baby waiting for his cleft lip to be fixed, the teenage girl who has just had her leg amputated racing in her wheelchair, the family teaching their son with cerebral palsy to walk, the mom pushing her daughter—shaved head and stitches from ear to ear—down to the lobby for a change of scenery, the baby with Down syndrome and a feeding tube sticking out of his nose being rocked to sleep. Such sights are around every corner.

And because such rare sights are the norm at Children's there doesn't need to be conversation about not calling other kids names. People don't stare at one another. Slurs and insults that would fly around the hallways at school and locker rooms before practice just don't find voice in Children's. That's because those who walk the halls have been on the receiving end of such hatred, they have children who are "different;" they themselves are "different;" they know what it's like to have something that no one else in their school has ever had to deal with. And so there's a camaraderie that develops, there's a kinship, there's a level of understanding, of familiarity with those who are other, or different. It makes Children's a model for what the world *could* be—God's kingdom on earth—a place where people actually "see" one another, respect one another for who they are, understand that everyone has their own story, and choose to see difference not as a joke to be exploited, but as a beauty to be celebrated.

The world could get to that place too. The need for movements like "Spread the Word to End the Word" (to remove the word "retard" in reference to people of differing intellectual abilities) could dry up, Public Service Announcements about the need to stop bullying would be a thing of the past, families refusing to go out for fear of their children being stared at would no longer need to worry; but as long as people keep their blinders on, the world still has a ways to go. As long as people think that the way to make themselves feel better is to put somebody who's different down, as long as Hollywood and television and advertising continue to perpetuate stereotypes and celebrate making jokes at others' expense, as long as the world remains "us" and "them" instead of "we," we're not going to make progress.

But then, it only takes one voice for progress to begin—or better yet, one afternoon sitting in the Children's Hospital lobby.

MARCH 18, 2008

An earlier update for all of you today, so you can get it while you're still at work! Today was a big day. Jacob came off oxygen—and seems to be doing quite well breathing the air the rest of us do. He also got his first bottle feed. It went slow, but pretty well. He was able to figure out the sucking, swallowing, and breathing thing to a point. But this will take some time. He's been fed without having to work for a good week now, so it will take some time for him to realize that he actually has to do something. And it will make him tired. Apparently babies burn quite a few calories while eating (if only the same thing happened for adults, right?). So now we're on to try the bottle every three hours.

The other good news is that Jacob had a chest x-ray this morning. This revealed that his heart is in better shape than before he had his surgery. Now you might think this would always be the case. However, sometimes when one thing is fixed in the heart, it can cause something also to stop working or to not work as well. So the good news is that Jacob's heart surgery did not cause anything else not to work. It actually made things work better. So that is good news indeed.

We're all doing well down here. We miss being home and being able to walk the journey of Holy Week with you, but as someone said in one of their messages to us, this certainly gives us a new perspective on Holy Week! It has been a holy, sacred week for sure.

I've added a couple more pictures for you to peek at. Just check out the onesie he is now able to wear! We're training him right for sure (in fact, I think he came early so he'd be home for opening day!). We will keep posting and we love reading all your messages— they have been such a boost to us while we've been away from you all. You are all in our prayers as I know we're in yours. Thank you so much for all you have done, and are doing for us. Until next time...

Tomorrow our world would change as we knew it. But not yet. Since we have a little time yet, I need to say a word about CarePages. CarePages is one of a couple of websites that allow patients to post updates on the health status of a family member or loved one. It is an amazing service that I stumbled across while I was reading some of the information Children's Hospital gave us before Jacob was born.

Being the pastor of a church, I am a public figure. There are many in the community who not only knew about what was happening with Kristen and our baby to be, but who were concerned and wanted updates. While e-mail is a blessing beyond all blessings (since even a preacher can't talk that much on the cell phone), the last thing I wanted to do after an exhausting day was to open up my e-mail and see an in-box with fifty or sixty messages in it. That would be enough to make me slam shut my laptop as quickly as I fired it up, and miss all the love and support that people were helpfully trying to send us. CarePages made that possible.

Each day, as you've seen and will see on the pages of this book, I posted an entry into CarePages. With the click of a button, everyone who subscribed to the page was sent an e-mail alerting them that our page had an update. They then simply needed to log on and read what I had written. No returning phone calls, no returning emails, no messages exaggerated or lost in translation (didn't you hear that Jacob actually had a twin sister whose heart was too big?). Just a simple webpage that had an impact on our lives that was anything but simple. Twenty-first century technology at its best.

For with each blog entry I wrote on CarePages, messages upon messages came back. Messages of love, messages of prayer, messages of hope. Funny messages, strange messages, even messages from people I really didn't know that well. They were words on a screen that turned into the hands that would uplift us and carry us on this journey in a way that we could never have imagined when we set off on it. There's a lot of research out there today suggesting that virtual communities are as important to people as face to face communities. Author Jesse Rice writes: "Younger generations, as well as an increasing number of people throughout the lifespan, would say relating in the "real" world is not an experience of either "higher" or "lower" quality [as compared to virtual communities], it is simply another way of relating."[3] I agree wholeheartedly. Although some might suggest that face-to-face interactions can never be replaced, these virtual messages and interactions were a close second. In fact, I can honestly say that they are what got me through.

Not only did my heart skip a beat with each message I read and with each log-in from our followers I witnessed (CarePages is a little big brother-ish, as the administrator can actually see who has logged on, and when—yeah, a little creepy, but actually very comforting), writing became a life line that I sorely needed. As a preacher and English major, I have often been known to process things and work through issues by putting pen to paper (actually, by putting fingers to keyboard). So this blog became cathartic for me. It gave me something to occupy my time during those long hours at the bedside. It was a way that I could laugh and cry through my words in a way that I couldn't seem to do otherwise. It had carried me through up until this point, and would be needed even more so when the world as we knew it changed: March 19, 2008, when Jacob was just nine days old.

Children's may have saved Jacob's life, but CarePages might just have saved mine.

MARCH 19, 2008

Good afternoon, everyone. It is a rainy day here in Boston (and probably snowing up north), but things continue to look bright for Jacob. He is still working on feeding, and seems to get better each time, but it's going to take some time for him to figure this all out, so we all have to be patient. Plus the fact, big brother Noah is spending the day here in the hospital with Jacob (so maybe he's a little distracted with Dora the Explorer playing in the background, I don't know). (By the way, Noah just loves looking at him!)

The big news, however, is that Jacob has been diagnosed with Down syndrome. We figured that this was the case, but were hoping, for Jacob's sake, that it wouldn't be. But he does have it. At this point it cannot be discerned how mild or severe a case it may be. This is something we'll see over time, as Jacob develops. Kristen and I are sad that this means that Jacob will have some additional struggles in life, but we are far from feeling sorry for ourselves. We know that with a child with special needs comes many, many special blessings—and we are convinced that he will make all of us better people for having him in our lives. We just can't wait to watch him grow into whatever his full potential may be (and possibly even medal at the Special Olympics… but we'll have to wait a while on that one!).

Other than that, things continue to progress. Jacob is real stingy about giving up his blood for tests, so the poor little guy has been stuck many, many times. He's certainly giving the doctors and nurses a run for their money. Except for when they are uncovering him to check him out or take some tests, he's incredibly peaceful. He sleeps soundly and has a little smirk-like smile on his face. We're just hoping that he remembers this when he gets back home!

We'll load some pictures up later this afternoon (we're hoping to convince Noah to hold him), and we'll try and do one written update a day—as we don't want to overburden you all with e-mail updates all the time! As always, thanks immensely to everyone for all your love, prayers, and support. And thanks to the Trustees and Deacons—your support of me taking the time I need before coming back to work is a real gift to all of us. Trust me when I say that I can't wait to get back to be with all of you, but I need to care for my family first before you'll get 100% from me. But I'm confident that you all can carry on without me and that all will be back to normal very soon.

We're hoping for more steps forward throughout the day and night ahead. Until next time…

It. Yup, that was the best word I had: it. Down syndrome. Not a chromosomnal (pretty sure I made that word up when I first tried to describe it) deficiency. Not a chromosomnal (yup, looked it up, I did make it up) abnormality. Not Down's Syndrome. Not Down Syndrome. But Down syndrome. Capital "D" and lowercase "s." Down syndrome. Two words that would change our lives in a far, far greater way than any of Jacob's heart concerns would. But we didn't know that then. In fact, the amazing thing about Down syndrome is that when we continue to think that it won't change our world any more, it keeps changing it. You'd think we'd have learned by now. But we're still learning. And I'm now convinced that this will be a lifelong process for us. But there are other Chapters to be told first.

So how did we find out? Well, Jacob was checked over by a physician on the night that he was born—looking for "markers" of Down syndrome. His almond-shaped eyes, protruding tongue, single crease across the center of his palm, and large space between his first and second toes seemed to indicate Down syndrome was a definite possibility—even to an untrained eye like mine. But whether that doctor knew that night, or not, we'll never know—since only a blood test can offer a definitive diagnosis, and he didn't offer an opinion. So blood work was sent off, and on March 19, they had come to give us the news.

Two young women approached us in Jacob's hospital room out on the "less intense" floor. They said that they had something to talk to us about. I probably should have known what was coming (especially since they took us into the Cardiac ICU waiting room), but I didn't. I blindly followed them back to what had been our old stomping grounds, politely chatting about an obscure theological book I was reading (which strangely one of the women had actually read).

They sat us down and in a very serious, yet compassionate, manner, they proceeded to tell us that Jacob had Down syndrome.

This was not the kind of Down syndrome that was genetically passed on (there were different kinds of Down syndrome?), but simply the cause of "something" that had happened when sperm fertilized egg. This meant that Noah would be no more at risk than anyone else of having a child with Down syndrome, and neither would we (Jacob, by virtue of his Down syndrome, is sterile, we'd find out later). Apparently this news was meant to allay our concerns, but since we didn't know to be concerned about it, it probably didn't have quite the desired effect they were looking for.

When the news came I remember that Kristen cried. I didn't. Very manly of me, right? No, not really. Actually, not at all. I don't think I really understood what those words meant. In fact, I'm still not sure I do (still learning, remember?) Kristen knew more than I. And she shed tears that day—not of pity or of anger—but of sadness for the challenges that our child was going to face—challenges that I couldn't yet have even begun to dream of.

They asked us if we had any questions. I did. I wanted to know if the heart condition caused the Down syndrome or vice versa. Really? That's what I asked? Yup. That was it. That's all I could think of. And when they told me that the Down syndrome had caused the heart condition, I wasn't sure whether to be relieved or not. I just wasn't sure about anything, except for one thing: I wasn't feeling sorry for myself. And I didn't see any need to ask God: Why?

I have never been of the opinion that God causes bad things to happen to people to punish them. I don't see God as the divine puppet master, deciding who gets what diseases and whose lives end far too early. I don't believe God works that way. Such a God is not consistent with my understandings of a God of love. Rather, I concur with many theologians who argue, convincingly, that those with differing abilities are not created that way because of the sins of their parents, as a punishment, or as a result of God's arbitrariness or capriciousness. Instead, I believe that we—differing abilities and all—are all created, uniquely, in the image of God.

But what is the image of God? Certainly not of a bearded old man, sitting with scepter in hand, on a throne of gold high in the clouds above. In fact, I don't view God as gendered or anthropomorphized at all. Rather, I think all such images, analogies, and metaphors that we can imagine of our Creator are inadequate attempts to explain the One who is beyond human understanding, description, or encapsulation.

We simply talk about God using human attributes, because we know of no other way. As theologian Alister E. McGrath helpfully notes: "Theology is 'talk about God.'" But how can God ever be described or discussed using human language? [Philosopher Ludwig] Wittgenstein made this point forcefully: "If human words are incapable of describing the distinctive aroma of coffee, how can they cope with something as subtle as God?"[4]

As such, these metaphors—while not explaining the entirety of God—become helpful means of recognizing, and speaking about, the various attributes of God. They are ways in which humanity has experienced God, or God has revealed God's self to humanity: as a father, as a mother, as a loving parent, etc. McGrath continues:

> *Divine self-revelation makes use of images and ideas which tie in to our world of everyday existence, yet which do not reduce God to that everyday world... Like all analogies, they break down at points. However, they are still extremely useful and vivid ways of thinking about God, which allow us to use the vocabulary and images of our own world to describe something which ultimately lies beyond it.*[5]

Such a view of God has given rise to many and varied theologies that envision God in ways that are helpful to, and speak to, the shared life experience of individuals. In the ancient world God was seen as a source of security from enemies, which led to the image of God as a father, ruling with a mighty hand, and the subsequent masculine language attributed to God in the pages of scripture. To a woman living in the twenty-first century a more helpful image might be of a mother, who can pick up a hurting child and hold her in loving arms that will not ever let go—an image that has given rise to feminist theological constructs of God as a woman.

All of this is not to say that we make God who we want God to be, but rather, that God—through the many and varied ways God reaches out to connect with us—has the ability to reveal God's self to us in ways that are as unique and varied as the individuals to whom God is being revealed. As such it becomes clear, through such revelations, that what makes us unique—imperfections included—gives God a unique and powerful access point to connect with us.

It's a feat that is accomplished, in no small part, because God chose to become one with humanity through the incarnation of Jesus Christ. It's an incarnation that gave God firsthand experience of what it's like to live and breathe, laugh and cry, feel joy and feel pain, just like each one of us. It's an incarnation that even enabled God, I would argue, to understand what it was like to live in an imperfect human body. For if Jesus was fully human—which I believe he was—then surely his body exhibited the characteristic imperfections that we all live our day-to-day lives with.

Given this experience, author Nancy L. Eiesland argues in her book *The Disabled God*, that God has firsthand knowledge of what it is like to live as a person of differing abilities. For Eiesland writes that Jesus became the exemplar of this "disability" (as she calls it, I prefer the term "differing ability"):

> *In presenting his impaired hands and feet to his startled friends, the resurrected Jesus is revealed as the disabled God. Jesus, the resurrected Savior, calls for his frightened companions to recognize in the marks of impairment their own connection with God, their own salvation. In so doing, this disabled God is also the revealer of a new humanity. The disabled God is not only the One from heaven but the revelation of true personhood, underscoring the reality that full personhood is fully compatible with the experience of disability.[6]*

Jesus then—living in an imperfect human body which was further marred by the disabling effects of crucifixion, and who led, what I would argue, was an imperfect life (the cursing of the fig tree in Mark 11:12–14 and his initial refusal to heal the Canaanite woman in Matthew 15:21–28 come to mind)—reveals that "disability not only does not contradict the human-divine integrity, it becomes a new model of wholeness and a symbol of solidarity."[7] Thus, this is to say that just as all of God's children envision a metaphor of God that speaks to them, they can also see a reflection of themselves in the person and body of God become human: Jesus—children with Down syndrome and other differing abilities not excepting.

Given this belief that we are all created in the image of God—the *Imago Dei*—I was never led to feel sorry for myself. I never asked: "Why me, God?" Why would I? Jacob was born imperfectly in the image of God who walked on this earth to experience imperfection just like the rest of us. It just so happened that Jacob's differences came in the form of a syndrome that I knew precious little about then. But that was no reason for me to feel sorry for myself or ask questions of God.

What I really should have been asking is: "How'd I get to be so lucky, God?" But I couldn't process that yet, either. At this point I knew very, very little about "it."

I know I said that I don't think God "caused" Jacob to have Down syndrome. It's true, I don't. Yet I have to say that two separate comments have me wondering. If nothing else (though it is certainly much more than this), Jacob's birth has made me revisit my theological understandings of the way God moves and works in this world. This is due in no small part to a colleague (who has a child with special needs) and our children's pediatrician, who both said to us that God selects special people to raise special children. I don't really buy that line of thinking, so I have never felt that Kristen and I were "chosen" specifically to parent Jacob. Yet a feeling I have had since before I was a father is enough to make me pause.

Before Noah was born I always had a feeling that I *wanted* a child who was "different" in my life. I didn't know what that meant and I still don't really know what that means, but I had a sense that two typically developing children was not to be, and should not be, the road for us. Part of me thinks that this was God's way of helping me get ready for the child who would be born to us; which is to say that even if God doesn't *cause* a child to be born with differing abilities, perhaps God has foreknowledge of when, and to whom, those children will be born. And as such, in a way that is not dissimilar to the way in which God calls people to ministry, or to service in the world, maybe God was "calling" me to become ready for what was to come, even if I was only vaguely hearing it, and understanding it even less.

Honestly, I don't know. I don't presume to know how God works. This is still one of those areas in process for me. And since I thoroughly believe that our theological understandings and beliefs should continue to change and be in process as we journey through life, I'm going to have to sit on this one and hope that maybe, someday, a new insight will come my way. I'm just not there yet.

But I am still listening, God.

A word about those two young women who gave us the news is also in order. A few weeks after that encounter in the Cardiac ICU waiting room I remember saying to Kristen: "Man, what an awful job those two have." But I'm not sure that's how they see it. They approached Kristen and me with the same compassion and tenderness that I try to approach those to whom I'm ministering, who have received bad news, or who are going through a tough time. They ministered to us—even though we didn't know it then.

And while we were blessed with many such doctors, nurses, and staff who would keep ministering to us in the days and weeks ahead, it bears mentioning that not all are so fortunate. There are horror stories out there of people who have been emotionally and spiritually abused by physicians who have done damage in the way they offered difficult news to patients and families. Uncaring, callous, and unsympathetic is no way to approach a family who is receiving life-changing news. Instead, whether you're Christian or Muslim, believer or nonbeliever, the words of Jesus fit: "You shall love your neighbor as yourself."

There's no need for a class (though there are great resources for doctors and others delivering a diagnosis of Down syndrome), no need for special talents—just a willingness to treat families the way that anyone would want to be treated if the roles were reversed and they were sitting across the table receiving the news about "it." Jesus' words in Matthew also come to mind here: "Truly I tell you, just as you did it to one of the least of these who are members of my family, you did it to me." In that case, Jesus was talking about his disciples giving food to the hungry, drink to the thirsty, welcoming the stranger, clothing to the naked, caring for the sick, and visiting those in prison. He told them that when they did these actions for a sister or brother on earth, they actually did those same actions for him. In our wilderness of confusion, little did we know then how hungry, thirsty, sick and alone, naked and imprisoned we were by the news we had just heard. And yet, those women found a way to respond to all our needs with some well-chosen words of compassion and well-timed hugs of empathy.

I had preached on this text countless times before, always envisioning myself as the food-giver, the caregiver, the visitor. But in that ICU waiting room, we were "the least of these," blessed that those women didn't need to hear a sermon about loving and caring for each and every child of God.

MARCH 20, 2008

Good afternoon everyone, and happy first day of spring! It's been an up and down day for us here in Boston. The good news is that Jacob continues to work at feeding. It's a very slow process, but each time he eats he seems to "get it" a little more. So we're just being patient and hoping that it just clicks for him sometime in the not too distant future.

We also received some good news today that Jacob's renal ultrasound (kidneys for the nonmedically literate) came back ok. They were concerned that something may be going on there due to some labs they drew, but according to the ultrasound his kidneys look all right. On the other hand, Jacob's platelets are inexplicably low. He has had a few transfusions of platelets, but they continue to read on the very low side. They are perplexed as to why this is happening, but they need to figure it out before they'll let Jacob come home. (This is being complicated due to the fact that Jacob is extremely hard to draw blood from.) Kristen and I even got some blood work done today in hopes that they might be able to come to some conclusion with our help! And I know that I speak for both of us when I say that we'd be happy to give every day if they could figure this out!

Other than that, we're doing fine. And I have to say, though we are away from our church home, in many ways we feel like we are walking this Holy Week journey with you all. At times it feels like the sadness of Maundy Thursday and Good Friday have settled down upon us, but then we remember that the joy of Easter is not too far behind—for soon we will be home with Jacob and experiencing the joy that we know he will bring to us all. Our prayer is that all of you will notice God walking beside you, as you journey through these next few days. For having experienced many of God's blessings here already—not to mention the tremendous love, support, and compassion from you all—we know that God is right here with us. Until next time…

Normally, on Maundy Thursday evening (three days before Easter Sunday), I would be leading a worship service in the Parish House of the church I serve. This is one of the most moving and meaningful services I have the privilege of presiding over each year. We pray together, share a potluck meal, and then hear, in different voices, the story of Jesus' final meal with his disciples, Judas' betrayal, the disciples' desertion, and Jesus' eventual crucifixion. The highlight of this service is always when we share communion together—a sacred and somber feast of remembrance. There would be no such meal for me this year, as I traded in bread and grape juice for the somewhat-less-sacramental cafeteria food.

The next time I stood up to serve communion, after returning to the church, it was a remarkably different experience. "Take. Eat. This is my body broken for you," I said preparing to share the loaf with the parishioners in the church; and yet, all I could think about was Jacob. A broken body. While I certainly would resist any label that suggested my son, or anyone with a differing ability, was "broken," this image of a body that was anemic when it came to giving blood, running low on platelets, and struggling to eat certainly felt less than whole. As such, hearing Jesus proclaim those words: "This is *my body, broken* for you" was—in a way that I had not anticipated—incredibly healing.

For in sharing that final meal, in praying earnestly for a different path than crucifixion, and in allowing his body to succumb to death on the cross, one could argue that Jesus was broken too—in body and in spirit. As Amos Yong writes in his book *Theology and Down Syndrome*: "the perennial Christian celebration of the life, death, and resurrection of Christ in the Eucharist…calls attention to the brokenness of the body of 'the disabled God.'"[8] And yet, this is "not as a demonstration of failure and defect," writes Nancy Eiesland, "but in affirmation of connection and strength."[9] It calls attention to the fact that God, in Jesus, understood what it meant to be a human being of differing abilities, and thus, as author Thomas Reynolds writes, Jesus' "disability indicates not a flawed humanity but a full humanity. Our bodies participate in the *imago Dei* in and through vulnerability and its consequent impairments not despite them."[10] Consequently, as children of God, made in God's image, those with differing abilities are able to commune with a God who looks, acts, sounds, and ambulates like them. As I held two halves of a broken loaf in my hands, my understanding started to become whole.

And if I understood, then how much more will those with differing abilities understand? To commune with a God who understands what our unique journey in life is like? Powerful. This is why it is a tragedy that some churches exclude those of differing abilities from making this sacred connection at the table—this, for "justifiable" reasons. In my view, the ability to sit quietly and wait for the bread and cup to be served, or to respond to the pastor with the proper words, or to eat without assistance, or to ambulate to the front of the church, or to ambulate to the front of the church *too soon*, should not be a barrier to receiving such a tangible symbol of God's blessing and grace. All should be—and in our congregation, all are—welcome to the table. It is a love feast, after all; and anything that places a barrier between a person and the table God sets for all God's children, in my view, is not a real celebration of communion.

These broken pieces began to come together in my mind as I held those broken pieces of bread. But I wouldn't really understand what all this meant until Jacob, unexpectedly, walked himself to the communion table during worship one Sunday. But that's a story that will have to wait to be told. For now, let me simply say that Jacob whetted my appetite for the sacrament in a way I had not expected. The juice just tastes sweeter and the bread richer now. Communion has never been—and will never be—the same in my eyes.

So why so much talk about the church and theology? Well, first, because this is my language. As a pastor and thus practical theologian, I think theologically. I can't help it, I just do. And, second, because I think that treatment of, and understanding of, persons with differing abilities is a matter that the church needs to focus some serious attention on. One example, though there are many, should suffice.

Author Brett Webb-Mitchell writes about a woman named Mary who had become exhausted looking for a church that could offer something to her family—and especially to her son Philip, who has Down syndrome:

> *"Tired of constantly asking and telling the church what to do, Mary took the counsel of a close friend, who also has a child with a disability. The friend told Mary to separate God from the church and not expect anything of the church. All her expectations should be placed on God, outside the context of the church. Since she has adopted this perspective, Mary says, she feels much better."*[11]

Mary may feel better, but this story makes me sad. Until every church not only welcomes Mary and Philip to their table—but goes out of their way to extend an *invitation* to them to commune—there's no doubt this conversation needs to continue, and the church has a lot of work left to do.

MARCH 21, 2008

When I was a kid (like many, I suppose), I always wondered why they would call Good Friday—the day Jesus died—"good." (I knew it wasn't just because we got a day off from school.) The best answer I got (even through my seminary years) was because this was the day that led to something good to come—Jesus' resurrection. I can only trust that when we look back on these days in the days and weeks to come, we will have a similar perspective and understanding. It's been a tough journey, with many blessings along the way, and even more to come, we know.

I also read in one of your posts that today is World Down Syndrome Day. Interesting that this day would fall on Good Friday this year. Something to think about, for sure…

Today has been a good day. Jacob's platelets have remained high—in the "normal" range. This is a good thing. The last platelet transfusion he got was over a day and a half ago. This means that his body hasn't immediately rejected the platelets. Hematology's plan is to draw blood from him on Monday and recheck the levels. If they are good, then they will continue to monitor, and it may just mean that it was a "transitory" thing. If they go down, I'm not sure what the next steps may be. It might mean a more invasive type of test. This is something we are really hoping doesn't have to happen— Jacob has already been poked and prodded enough for a lifetime. So we'll keep our fingers crossed that those platelets remain up.

We're also happy to report that Jacob had a good chest X-ray today. His heart continues to look good. As far as feeding goes, he is maintaining where he was yesterday. He eats some, gets tired, and then needs to have the rest fed to him. Again, we're just hoping that one of these days it all just clicks for him. They also mentioned, for the first time, that it's possible for him to go home on a feeding tube (to supplement the oral feedings we're giving him)—but that's something to be decided further down the road.

Other than that we're doing well. I made it back home yesterday long enough to restart our furnace (the house was mighty cold), grab a few things, sleep, and go for a run this morning. It was good to be home—and I can't wait until all four of us get to be there for good. Your notes continue to inspire us. We really are doing well, and we love the fact that you are so interested in walking this journey with us. Every day when we see the number of hits this website gets continue to rise, our spirits are lifted. It would surely be a lonely road without your company. So thank you, from the bottom of our hearts, for your support.

We've added a few new pictures (none as cute as Jacob and Noah together, but they're something to look at). Until next time…

Thirst. Think of the last time you were thirsty, and I mean *really* thirsty. You'd just finished playing an hour's worth of soccer in the scorching afternoon sun; you'd stood up in front of the church to read some words of remembrance at your mother's funeral; you'd finally made the left-hand turn from Hereford Street to Boylston, and the finish line of the Boston Marathon was mercifully in sight. Thirsty. Thirsty in body and thirsty in spirit.

Is it any wonder that one of the phrases Jesus uttered from the cross on that Good Friday was "I thirst"? He thirsted in body and spirit for the journey to finally be finished. He thirsted for the culmination.

I was thirsty, too, on Good Friday. But I had no idea what would quench my thirst. For better platelet level counts? For Jacob to start feeding? To understand what World Down Syndrome Day would mean for my family? For part of Jacob's journey in this the world to go smoothly? For a morning that didn't start with a trip past the bouncing and rolling balls in the Children's Hospital lobby? I wasn't sure. I just knew I was thirsty.

Little did I know that Easter, just two days away, would provide the resurrecting refreshment I sorely needed.

MARCH 23, 2008

I have to say, if you had asked me six months ago what Easter Sunday was going to be like, I never—in my wildest dreams—would have imagined this. Instead of worshipping side by side with a house full of my brothers and sisters, singing joyful Easter hymns, and smelling the overpowering aroma of lilies, I'm sitting in a quiet hospital room, with the sun shining brightly at my back (making the computer screen hard to see), watching little Jacob doze off to sleep. It certainly does give me a new perspective on the joy of Easter, and I know now that I will never look at Easter the same way again. But as hard as it is for me to be away from my spiritual home, I know that this is where I need to be, with the resurrected Christ very much with us in this holy place.

I didn't post yesterday because it was a quiet day. Lots of family in to visit, and no tests for Jacob at all. He got a bath, we learned about how to care for all of his incisions, and Jacob worked at feeding. He is getting better. He took 14 milliliters of food orally last night. While that's not a whole lot, it's a big jump from the 2–4 milliliters he was taking just a couple of days ago. So we continue to see signs of progress.

Tomorrow will be a big day. Jacob will have his blood tested again. We're hoping that his platelet numbers will remain high. If that's the case, then we will likely start talking about coming home (yeah!). If they are low, we're not sure what the next steps will be. So we're trying not to think about the latter—we're just hoping his numbers look good. We anticipate another quiet day today. The weekend tends to be a little slower around here. Some more family will be in to celebrate Jacob's first Easter with us, so that will be fun.

And so we'll just wait and see how tomorrow goes. I wish you all a very happy and blessed Easter Sunday. May you experience the resurrected Christ in your midst today, and may that presence cause you to share the love you feel with all your brothers and sisters around you. Believe me, through your words, and the work of the folks here at Children's, we have felt God closer than we could have ever imagined, and if that's not a sign of the resurrected Christ in our midst, then I don't know what is.

Alleluia! Christ is risen, Christ is risen indeed! With Easter joy in your hearts, may your life bring joy to others, today and always. (Don't forget to check out the pictures, including a special one for Easter Sunday!) Until next time…

Two and a half years after this post was completed, I decided to share it in one of my sermons—my *Thanksgiving* sermon, believe it or not. Here's what I had to say:

"What I am saying, though, is that I think there is something to be gained—something that we might be missing—in not having an opportunity to share stories of the ways in which God has been at work in our lives, the ways in which we have noticed God, felt God's presence, and sensed God speaking to us, you might say, that have impacted our lives.

And so, rather than just saying this, I want to show you what I mean by offering a little from my own life and experience. One of the most profound moments of sensing God's presence in my life came on Easter Sunday, 2008. Since it was Easter, you'd assume that it was a moment right here in this sanctuary, but it wasn't. For that Easter I wasn't with you, because it was just 13 days after our second son Jacob had been born. As such, I was spending Easter morning, with Jacob, at Boston Children's Hospital, while Kristen and Noah visited with our family.

Coming just four days after Jacob had been diagnosed with Down syndrome, amid all kinds of post-op tests and procedures, my emotions were all over the place—in no small part due to the fact that I wasn't worshiping on Easter Sunday, but was sitting in a hospital room. You may recall that during that time I was keeping people posted on CarePages, as to what was happening with Jacob.

[Here, I read the first paragraph from my CarePage post above, before continuing.] *There was something about that morning, that space, the feel of the sun on my back, watching Jacob sleep, that helped me know, for certain, that God was with me in that place, and that, regardless of what happened, we were going to be okay. That morning was one of the single most religious experiences of my life—one that still brings tears to my eyes today.*

I share it with you now simply to say that I think our lives would be richer if we did more of this. Again, I'm not talking about sharing conversion stories—because that's foreign to many of us— but simply stories of the ways in which we have felt God working and moving and speaking in our lives. What would it be like to share those? What could we learn about one another? How could our relationships be deepened? And what could we learn about the ways God works in the world by hearing how God has worked in the lives of our sisters and brothers?"

I learned that when we need be refreshed, God is there, holding the cup—giving us drinks we didn't know we needed of liquids we didn't know existed. As the Psalmist so eloquently writes, God was giving us "drink from the river of [God's] delights."[12] With Jacob's introduction into our lives, those drinks would be abundant.

Alleluia and Amen.

Time to let a few of the CarePage entries speak for themselves.

MARCH 24, 2008

So I know everyone has been anxious to hear about the platelet count. (Platelets help to clot blood, in case you're interested.) Well, Jacob has decided not to cooperate so far by not giving enough blood to be tested today. They will try again tonight, but were unsuccessful this morning. The good news is, however, that hematology has led us to believe that we'll be able to monitor his platelets in an outpatient setting (either with our cardiologist or pediatrician). Apparently there is new research out which suggests that 66% of babies with Down syndrome have low platelet counts, and so that's their best guess as to what's causing this. It's hematology's belief that the body will rectify this problem over time—it just takes a little longer in babies with Down syndrome. But they basically told us that since Jacob is not due for surgery for a few months, they will not hold us here because of the platelet count. Whew!

So now we just need to get Jacob eating by mouth and gaining weight. They've started to suggest that Thursday might be the day for us to head home, with us continuing to supplement Jacob's feedings with a feeding tube. In fact, they are already calling some companies up our way to see if we can get the equipment we'll need at home. That's good news indeed! But first Jacob has to keep improving with his feeds, and start gaining a little more weight. He's still very tiny, and they want to make sure he's on track by getting bigger.

We're doing well. It's hard to believe that Jacob was born two weeks ago. What a whirlwind of events have transpired since then! We continue to be ever so grateful for all your love and support. We'll keep you posted on how the feeding is going and what his platelet count is (whenever they can test them!). Until next time...

MARCH 25, 2008

Wow has it ever been busy around here today! That's good news, because we're starting to get things in place for going home. Yeah! We met with a woman who showed us how to use the pump to feed Jacob, we have had conversations about medicine and bathing, we were told that Jacob passed his car seat test (yes, they actually test now to make sure that they can sit in a car seat for an hour and a half), and we've talked about all kinds of follow-up outpatient appointments. But the fact that they are talking about outpatient is wonderful news!

Jacob will be reevaluated by his cardiologist tomorrow morning. If the cardiologist gives his ok, we'll likely be coming home on Thursday. The platelet count came in late last night, and although it was low, it's not so low that Jacob needs a transfusion. Again, good news. He'll be monitored by hematology as an outpatient as well, with the hopes that it will rectify itself over time (although they are still running other tests).

Other than that, we're doing well. We are very excited to be talking about coming home, and are hopeful that it will be on Thursday. It will be great to get back into our familiar space and let Jacob learn how to feed in the comforts of his own home.

So that's it for now. I'll try to get some new pictures up within the next day or so. So please keep those prayers coming, and we look forward to letting you see Jacob for yourselves (not just in cyberspace) real soon! Until next time...

MARCH 26, 2008

Well…maybe not Thursday. The cardiologist came in this morning to take a peek at Jacob. They'd like him to stay for a "few" more days just to see him consistently gain weight, eat more, and get his breathing under control (with the mixing blood in his heart, he breathes fast from time to time). So, we're back in the waiting game again. It could be Friday, Saturday, or perhaps next week. We don't know just when yet.

But for the most part Jacob is doing well. Cardiac-wise the surgery was a great success. The repair to his aorta looks good. He remains on medicine to help remove some of the fluid from around his heart (this is normal for "cardiac kids" as they call them). So he'll remain on that for some time, for sure. Hematology will also be drawing yet another set of labs on him before he goes home. If the platelets have dropped lower, they will need to transfuse him one more time. Then we will monitor his levels on an outpatient basis.

So I guess if Jacob were playing for the Red Sox, you might say that he's day to day. We'll come in, talk with the doctors, and then see which day will be the best for him to come home. Of course, we'll keep you posted. And, as always, continued thanks for all of your support—you'll get to see Jacob one of these days, trust us! Until next time….

MARCH 27, 2008

Well, not a whole lot to update you on today. Jacob isn't coming home today; we know that for sure. No-one has said when yet. Perhaps tomorrow, but more than likely sometime after that. We're actually not too frustrated with this. We want him to be where he's going to get the best care possible—and if that means a few more days in Boston, then that's what it means. We're just trying to work out all the other logistics that come with being away from home for so long. But we're managing! (And thank you to everyone for being so understanding!)

Jacob is still working at feeding. Last night he didn't gain or lose weight. Good that he didn't lose, but we'd really love to see him start packing on the pounds! (This is one of those few instances in life when you actually root for someone to gain weight!) He's also getting a blood transfusion of platelets. This wasn't unexpected. His count was very, very low when they drew labs today. So he's getting the transfusion and will continue to be monitored here in the hospital and on an outpatient basis when he leaves. Again, it's a problem that's associated with Down syndrome and should remedy itself sometime in the future.

You know... I'm feeling like I should give some substance to this update today, so I'm thinking that I'll share something with you called "Welcome to Holland." Since hearing Jacob's diagnosis of Down syndrome, probably 10 people have told us about this. It's by Emily Perl Kingsley, and it has certainly offered us some food for thought as we've been journeying over the past two and a half weeks. And so I'll share it with you now...

"I'm often asked to describe the experience of raising a child with a disability—to try to help people who have not shared that unique experience to understand it, to imagine how it would feel. It's like this......

When you're going to have a baby, it's like planning a fabulous vacation trip - to Italy. You buy a bunch of guide books and make your wonderful plans. The Coliseum. The Michelangelo David. The gondolas in Venice. You may learn some handy phrases in Italian. It's all very exciting.

After months of eager anticipation, the day finally arrives. You pack your bags and off you go. Several hours later, the plane lands. The stewardess comes in and says, "Welcome to Holland."

"Holland?!?" you say. "What do you mean Holland?? I signed up for Italy! I'm supposed to be in Italy. All my life I've dreamed of going to Italy."

But there's been a change in the flight plan. They've landed in Holland, and there you must stay.

The important thing is that they haven't taken you to a horrible, disgusting, filthy place, full of pestilence, famine, and disease. It's just a different place.

So you must go out and buy new guide books. And you must learn a whole new language. And you will meet a whole new group of people you would never have met.

It's just a <u>different</u> place. It's slower-paced than Italy, less flashy than Italy. But after you've been there for a while and you catch your breath, you look around.... and you begin to notice that Holland has windmills....and Holland has tulips. Holland even has Rembrandts.

But everyone you know is busy coming and going from Italy... and they're all bragging about what a wonderful time they had there. And for the rest of your life, you will say "Yes, that's where I was supposed to go. That's what I had planned."

And the pain of that will never, ever, ever, ever go away... because the loss of that dream is a very, very significant loss.

But... if you spend your life mourning the fact that you didn't get to Italy, you may never be free to enjoy the very special, the very lovely things ... about Holland."[13]

Until next time…

Duh! We should have known. Mine and Noah's favorite color is orange. (Translation, for all the nonsoccer fans out there: Holland's national soccer team wears orange, because that is the color of the Dutch royal family.) Something tells me we should have been planning for a trip to Holland all along. But alas, we, too, got to understand— firsthand—the unexpectedly blessed detour that comes with living a life with a child with differing abilities. A detour that can be found, not just in the birth of the child, but in many of the myriad of curves life throws at us. I shared as much in a sermon I preached one Sunday.[14] Here's a portion of it:

> *What that Holland story does, however, is to put some perspective on [our life] situation. It helps us to recognize that though the wilderness experience is painful—because none of us want to find out that our children are anything less than perfect— and though it does leave a lingering wound, there is still a blessing to be had from the experience—if you're open to receiving it.*
>
> *It's true for those of us who have children with disabilities, but it's no less true for those of you who have had other wilderness moments in your lives. Perhaps it was the death of a loved one, a divorce, or the time when your children left home leaving you with an empty nest. Maybe it was a forced change of a job, or a spell on unemployment. Or it might have been a difficult battle with cancer, a serious illness that landed you in the hospital for some time, or watching your child struggle through a difficult period.*
>
> *Whatever it may be, I think it's fair to say that we have all had those wilderness moments in our lives—those extremely tough times when things don't go according to the plans we had, or that cause us to turn our lives in a whole new direction. These are tough times that can scar us both literally and figuratively.*
>
> *But, remember what we said earlier, there's also a blessing to be had from those experiences. For while I do not believe that God causes us to go through these wilderness moments in our lives, I do believe that God meets us in those wilderness places, engages us in that tussle of faith we so often find ourselves in while we're there, and then bestows a blessing upon us—even though we might not be able to see it for years to come. Through all that wrestling, through all that pain, through all that sadness, through all that hardship, there is a blessing to be had.*
>
> *It's a blessing that can be attributed only to the grace of God. But remember that this isn't "grace as it's usually imagined. [It's] not sweet 'amazing grace.' [This is] tough assaulting grace."[15] It's a grace-full blessing that is only received by struggling and wrestling with God through whatever experience has befallen us. An experience that changes us, and perhaps… perhaps… even changes God.*
>
> *And so, my friends, I hope you'll hear this message today. Whether you've been through the wilderness in the past, whether*

you're in the deep depths of the woods now, or whether you can see that dark thicket of trees approaching on the horizon, remember what you've heard today: even in the wilderness, God's blessings are to be had.

For even though we often tussle with God while we're there— angry and frustrated with whatever has befallen us—which is a perfectly faithful response to a trying time, I do believe that through God's graciousness, blessings will emerge from our wilderness wrestling, even though it may not seem like it in the heat of the battle.

Which is to say that we would all do well to keep striving, keep journeying, keep wrestling, and keep the faith—remembering that God's wilderness blessings will surely follow. Amen.

It's often said that no preacher preaches a sermon that he or she doesn't need to hear. And I certainly needed a reminder that God's blessings were to be had in the wilderness, in Holland, and in Boston Children's Hospital. Even—and especially—on Thanksgiving.

MARCH 28, 2008

Short update today because we're going home! Yeah! Woohoo! We just got word from the folks here at Children's. We're doing the whole discharge thing, so it might take a little while, but we'll be headed out before the day is through. (Whether we make it all the way up north, however, is another story—as we hear there's quite a little snow storm going on up there! But nevertheless, we'll be back in our own home by tomorrow morning at the latest if the weather is too bad to get there tonight!)

So, that means that this CarePage will not be getting updated as regularly as it has been. But fret not, we will still be posting pictures here periodically, and giving periodic updates, so feel free to keep visiting and leaving us messages. Also, this will be the page we will use when Jacob comes back in for his next surgery or surgeries (hopefully the former). So keep the site and your password handy— we'll be using it again soon!

So that's it for today. Thank you so much for your love, prayers, and support—it has been amazing! We are forever indebted to you all for all you have given us. And the best part is, you'll all be able to meet Jacob, in the flesh, sometime very soon!

Until next time…

The moment we had all been waiting for had arrived! Chapter one (or eighteen, who's really counting?) had finished. Our flight may have been delayed leaving the terminal in Boston, but we were ready to soar to our destination, knowing that we would be making many return trips back in the months and years to come. For now we were headed home: Maine, Holland—it didn't matter—we just wanted to be together, under one roof, again. And that's where we were headed.

God's unexpected—and thoroughly welcome—wilderness blessings were raining down all over us. We were finally beginning to see them and feel them. And it felt good.

MARCH 31, 2008

As that great theologian Dorothy Gale said so eloquently, "There's no place like home!" It is great to be back in our house, finally. Kristen, Noah, Jacob, and I enjoyed a very nice weekend together. We're starting to settle into a routine already. With feedings every three hours, we're feeling a bit sleep deprived (especially since we have to set an alarm to wake Jacob up to feed!), but that's ok. We want him to be as big as possible for his next surgery. And it looks like we're on the right track. Jacob was weighed by his pediatrician today, and he's 5 pounds, 1 ounce. That is good news. We just hope he keeps getting bigger and stronger over the weeks ahead.

I will plan to add some more pictures this evening. Just so you know, you won't get an email when we add photos to the site (just when we add text), so feel free to check back in to see what's new with the photo gallery. We'll try to keep the written updates to a minimum while Jacob is home, but will be sure to keep you posted on his progress. And we'll be sure to add photos from time to time.

Jacob is off to see his cardiologist and the hematologist later this week. (FYI, his latest platelet levels as taken on Monday were higher than they were after the transfusion in the hospital! This might mean that his body is no longer breaking down the platelets. So he might have licked that issue. We'll just have to wait and see...) Hopefully, all will go well with all the visits. Continued thanks for your love, support, and prayers. It was especially great to have Jacob meet his new church family yesterday—what a thrill for us all.

As I said, photos to come tonight (I hope!). Until next time...

So it turns out the trip to Holland wasn't that bad after all—though the reality of life in Holland took some getting used to, just like the wilderness. Jacob came home on a feeding tube. This meant that he had a long yellow tube that went in through his nose and down into his stomach. The end outside his body was taped to his face, and had a little clear cap on it which swung around like an extra appendage. A few times each day, after feeding Jacob, we would hook him up to a machine. We'd pour formula into a bag, check the settings, snake the tube through the feeding machine, and then sit as Jacob lay in bed—often asleep—as the rest of the nourishment he needed filled his body.

For mothers who breastfeed, I've heard that that bond between mother and child, eye to eye, skin on skin, is unlike any other. This was just a bit different. Late night feedings for us meant watching Jacob doze off in his crib, while the whirr of a feeding machine sang us both a lullaby. In the end there was no burping, no trying to place the baby back into the crib without waking him; just a simple unhooking of the feeding tube, a trip to the sink to wash out the feeding bag, and back to bed while Jacob snoozed away.

This wasn't the only way life in the "real world" took some getting used to, though. Remember Walmart? (Now I have to say that I am not a fan of Walmart. Their history of unfair treatment of workers and of coming into a community, lowering prices (so as to knock their competitors out of business), and then raising prices back up is disgraceful. Just watch the film "Walmart: The High Cost of Low Price" to see for yourselves.) We avoid Walmart when at all possible. Yet, with mounting medical bills and two small children, sometimes, inexplicably, we just find ourselves walking through those doors.

When Noah was a baby, Kristen recalls walking through Walmart one day only to see an older woman approach the baby carriage (as those with children know, older people love to come up and admire little babies). Yet this was fairly out of the ordinary. Instead of commenting on how cute Noah was, or asking how old he was, this woman asked if she could sniff his head. Yes, you read that right, a total stranger coming up and asking if she could sniff our baby's head. Babies have that special smell to them, I understand that, but this request…well… let's just say that while Kristen doesn't recall what she said, it's safe to say that there was no head-sniffing allowed.

Now compare that to the older woman (the same, perhaps?) who had nothing to say when she peered into Jacob's car seat years later.

Yup. It was the feeding tube that got her. People just aren't used to sticking their heads into a carriage and seeing anything but the perfect resemblance of the Gerber baby. The feeding tube was just too much for this woman, and she didn't know how to respond. So she didn't. And I'll admit that it hurt. It hurt to think that Jacob's differences made him, somehow, uncute or unlovable.

We'd get over it, though. I couldn't articulate it then, but I began to realize that such a reaction actually says more about that woman than it does about Jacob. As a friend of mine says, "We all have our challenges and our shit to deal with. It's just that, for Jacob, that shit is visible on the outside."

Today we just laugh such reactions off and in so doing, feel sorry for people like that lady. Being so stuck inside her own box, she's missing out on a pretty amazing world with some pretty amazing people in it. Translation: If you're only sniffing the heads of perfect people, you've got a whole lot of sniffing left to do.

APRIL 4, 2008

So, just a quick update now that we have been home for a week!
The four of us are beginning to settle into a routine as we recall
what it's like to be up every three hours to feed! But that's ok. Jacob
is doing well, eating more, and gaining weight—those are all very
good things.

During the many appointments Jacob had this week, two new
bits of news came out. The first is that Jacob's platelets are fine!
He has had two blood tests done since leaving the hospital and the
platelets have gone up both times! This likely means that the low
platelet numbers were simply due to his having Down syndrome.
They should, we are told, remain up from here on out as his body
has figured out how to regulate them. We'll get another blood test in
a month, but they are confident that things will be fine.

And secondly, Jacob has seen his cardiologist up north. She
is very nice—we like her a lot. She will now monitor Jacob about
every two weeks. We need to watch for changes in his breathing,
him getting more tired, eating less, etc. As we watch and as she
observes him, we will make the call as to when surgery will happen.
And that's when they'll decide, once and for all, whether or not they
can fix the heart, or whether he'll need the 2-3 surgery route. We're
hoping for the former, and they're optimistic that can happen, but
we'll just have to wait and see for sure in a couple of months.

That's all for now. Thanks so much for the continued prayers.
More pictures soon, we promise! Until next time…

For all that that woman in Walmart wasn't, Jacob's cardiologist was. From the moment we walked into that office, we were treated the way all new parents should be. The staff and receptionist came out from around the desk and admired Jacob appropriately (in other words, *a lot*). They kept telling us how cute he was and how amazing he was doing—reminding us, again, how blessed we are. But just the same, this still was life in the wilderness. This wasn't a "healthy baby" checkup (or whatever they call those routine, post-birth doctor's office visits). This was a time for heart monitoring, oxygen saturation level checking, and an extensive echocardiogram—all-too-common trail markers for us in the wilderness.

And yet, the cardiologist and her staff were the perfect trail guides. They had a block of time—three hours, or so—set aside for us to do the tests and procedures they needed to do, yes, but also to make sure that we had an opportunity to ask questions and get the answers we'd been looking for. This office may have been fifty miles or so north of Boston, but it felt, very much, like we were back in the competent, caring, and capable hands of Children's Hospital.

Not all of our interactions with doctors, specialists, therapists, and the like, would be as positive, though. And we know that will be the case as we move with Jacob in the future. Our cardiologist was "the way life should be" (to steal a Maine moniker), but life so often isn't for families of children with differing abilities.

With a life of early intervention, occupational therapy, physical therapy, speech therapy, mainstreaming and inclusion meetings, and the marking of birthdays with Individualized Education Plans (IEPs), we have come to know how important those professional relationships are. Although it has been a learning curve for us, advocacy has become a big word in our house. We know now that if we don't advocate for Jacob, then no one else will. We are the best ones to ensure that the educational system makes a difference in Jacob's life so that he has a better chance at making a difference in the world.

We haven't been—and we won't be—perfect, but it's a high calling and responsibility that we have vowed to never neglect.

APRIL 10, 2008

A very brief update for you tonight. Jacob is doing very well. He's up to 5 pounds, 8 ounces! He has also taken 4 or 5 complete feeds with his bottle (that means we didn't need to supplement with his feeding tube). That's all good news.

Jacob is continuing to see his cardiologist, visiting nurses have been checking up on him, and all looks good. He has only managed to pull his feeding tube out once (that was fun!). And he continues to sleep well for us and watch his big brother run around the house. Our cardiologist is suggesting that by the end of May we may have a sense of when (and what) Jacob's next surgery/surgeries may be.

The four of us have certainly settled into a routine here at home. We're a little sleep deprived, but it's been fun for us all to be together as a family. Thank you so much for all your love, prayers, and support. And thank you especially to our church family for all the wonderful meals that have been sent our way! We really appreciate it.

Check out the picture gallery (yes, we've finally added some new photos!). Until next time…

APRIL 28, 2008

Wow. It's hard to believe that it's been two weeks since our last update! Apologies. Time certainly flies now that we're back home, at work, living life, and squeezing in a celebration of Noah's 3rd birthday.

So here's where we are. Jacob weighed in at 6 pounds 2 ounces a little over a week ago. He's pretty much taking 6 feeds a day completely by mouth (with some exceptions, of course), and then he receives two feeds overnight through the feeding tube. We're assuming that the tube will stay in until after Jacob's surgery, but we'll find out more next week when he goes to meet with the feeding team.

For now, the big news we're awaiting is Jacob's cardiology appointment this Friday. At that appointment he'll have an echocardiogram. This will go a long way toward telling us two things: 1) what type of surgery Jacob will be having; and 2) when that surgery might be. We're not getting our hopes up, but we're optimistic that they'll be able to repair his heart in just one surgery. But we will see (and certainly keep you posted).

Other than that, life is good for us. We've adjusted quite well to having all four of us at home. We've certainly appreciated the many meals that have come from our church family—it has been a tremendous blessing to us. Noah likes Jacob quite a bit (he's very fond of singing to him—"Take Me Out to the Ballgame" especially!). Believe it or not, it's actually hard to think back to what life was like with just three of us!

So thank you all for your continued prayers and support. We've added more pictures to the site and we'll keep updating periodically (with the updates coming more frequently when we close in on Jacob's next surgery). Until next time…

Noah: the big brother. I confess that when I first heard about Jacob's heart problems, diagnosis of Down syndrome, and all that, one of my first thoughts was of Noah. At almost three years old, he didn't ask for this. He didn't ask for a brother who would spend so much time in the hospital. He didn't ask for a nearly three-week stay at his grandparents' house after Jacob was born (and a similarly lengthy stay to come). He didn't ask for a life in which Mom and Dad would always be asking him to be careful of Jacob's feeding tube when he holds him. But that's what he got. And I admit that I felt sorry for Noah. He wouldn't have, I thought (and have already been proven wrong), that little brother to play tricks on, to wrestle with, or to play soccer against in the backyard—that little brother who would smash all his carefully crafted Lego creations. He didn't ask for Jacob, but that's who he got. And you know, despite my feelings, I think Jacob is exactly who Noah wanted.

At not quite three years old, Noah didn't understand what Down syndrome meant. We told him that it would take Jacob a little longer to learn how to do things than it might take some other kids. We told him that just like a cut on your arm needs some medicine and a bandage to get better, Jacob's heart needed to be similarly made better. We know he didn't understand all of this…or did he?

While Noah has never been a rough and tumble child, he is still a young boy. And yet, his demeanor around Jacob is nothing like I would expect from a boy his age. He hugs Jacob. He holds Jacob tenderly. He sings to him. He reads to him. He wants to be with him. He is, if I didn't know any better, almost protective of his little brother in a way that I'm not sure many siblings are. He understands that the rules need to be a little different when it comes to Jacob, and yet, he takes it all in stride.

I was worried that Noah's life would be detrimentally impacted by the birth of his baby brother with special needs. I couldn't have been more wrong. Noah has shown me that, in no uncertain terms, he was ready to have Jacob as his sibling. Noah needed Jacob. And I know for Jacob the feelings are mutual when he stares into the caring, blue eyes of his favorite person in the world.

Yet Noah's reaction hasn't been the only one to surprise me. I was also worried about our family. How would they react to the news that they now had a person with differing abilities who would be present at Easter and Thanksgiving, who wouldn't understand how to open Christmas presents until he was much older (still waiting….), who might slow us down if we all took a trip to Fenway Park together, who would make taking family pictures more of an effort than it usually is (true to form, Jacob is already a champ at this), who would have an oxygen cord to mirror his great-grandmother's trailing him around at family gatherings? How would they react? I was worried.

Again, I needn't have been. They, equaling Noah's reaction, took it all in stride—as if Jacob was the relative they had been expecting, as if they knew we were headed to the wilderness all along and, as such, already knew what life would be like for us there and were prepared to show us around a bit. Because the reality is, whether our shit is visible on the outside or hidden on the inside, I think you'd be hard pressed to find anyone with children who hasn't spent time mucking around, lost in the wilderness.

Though he'd never say it, Jacob has a bond with Kristen's father that I've never seen before; Kristen's mother—not an overtly religious person—had a candle in their window burning every night while Jacob was in the hospital; my mother's lap just seems to attract an eager-to-play-patty cake Jacob more frequently than I remember any of the other grandkids; and my Dad shocked me by telling me that his dream has always been to work with the Special Olympics. They'll tell you they don't play favorites, yet they all seem quite at home showing us around in the wilderness—this, as we were wondering whether we were going to be forced to navigate those often-bleak woods all alone.

Our siblings, Jacob's cousins, and the extended family have been no different. I was worried that Jacob would somehow be resented, or be burdensome, or that we would no longer be as welcome at those family gatherings which mean the world to us. And yet, if anything, Jacob draws people together instead of pulling people apart—a gift that, I believe, we will continue to see blossom in this world as he gets older.

Who knew? I couldn't have been more wrong. And they couldn't have been more right.

Just a couple of years later—when Jacob was three and Noah was in first grade—Noah came home from school with a book he had chosen to read as his homework. The book was titled *Leo the Late Bloomer*. Without even being asked why he chose it, Noah offered: "I chose it because it reminds me of Jacob. The lion in the story just takes a little bit longer to learn stuff."

Yeah, I'd say Jacob is the sibling Noah wanted. And for Jacob I know the feeling is mutual.

MAY 2, 2008

Hold your horses—two updates in a week that Jacob is not in the hospital—uncharted territory, I know! But we figured we'd pass along the latest since I know many of you are wondering about Jacob's trip to the cardiologist today.

Let me first just say that we're moving into the time when the medical jargon far surpasses my ability to comprehend or to pass on to all of you—so bear with me here. The basic thing we heard today was that it's still a little premature to put a game plan into place. Jacob's heart is very complex, and so they are watching a number of different factors interplay. They're watching his breathing, his feeding, how his lungs are developing, how his small right ventricle is developing, how his heart valves are working, where the blood is flowing, where the blood is not flowing, how much oxygen is going where, etc. (See what I mean about this being complex?) So right now they are still monitoring all those things. Since Jacob has not changed much since his last visit, there's no need to jump into anything just yet, so they're going to wait and see a little longer before deciding. This is really a crucial decision, because once they decide on a plan, they can't change course 2 or 3 years down the line. So they want to get it right when they make their decision.

They did mention a couple things to us. Apparently there are three types of repairs they're looking at here: a two ventricle, a one-and-a-half ventricle, and a one ventricle repair. Our doctor didn't get into the specifics of each one, but said that a two ventricle repair is best. She's not 100% confident that he will be able to have such a surgery, but she's not saying he can't either. In fact, she said that it might be that a decision is made once they're in for surgery—and it will be the surgeon's call. She did say that she was meeting with Jacob's Boston cardiologist and the surgeon next Tuesday, and they will be talking about Jacob—so perhaps we'll learn more after that.

They also mentioned the possibility of a cardiac catheterization. This is the first time we've heard this. This is a one day procedure (where Jacob would be in the hospital overnight), and it will give them a good look at how blood is flowing, how his lungs are working, etc. This is a very real possibility as they seek to gain more data.

As far as everything else goes, Jacob is up to 6 pounds, 7 ounces. This is good, but a little behind where they'd like to see him. So we will be meeting with a feeding team next week to see if his caloric intake needs to be upped. His oxygen saturation level is in the mid-80s. This is about where he's been and actually a good sign. Too low or too high, even, are not good signs. So mid-80s is good.

So I guess that's all we know for now. Hopefully in a couple weeks we'll have more of a game plan for you. We're guessing that surgery will happen in June or July, now, but that's just a real wild guess—no one knows for sure.

Thanks so much for the support and prayers and keep them coming. We'll take all that we can get! Until next time...

The big day turned out to be not so big after all. We were looking for answers and plans and surgery dates, and we got a lot more "Well, we'll just have to wait and see what happens." More uncertainty—a characteristic of life in the wilderness. But where there was uncertainty, there was also certainty—coming, in large part, from our church family.

Now my hope in this book is not to convince you to become a believer, or to join a church (though if you're looking, the United Church of Christ is worth checking out!), but I do have to testify to my experience—and that is, we wouldn't have made it through without our church community. After arriving home we were blessed with meal after meal arriving on our doorstep (an intricately planned operation I learned after the fact, of mostly other young families sending us meatballs and lasagna and anything else that could be easily frozen and reheated for meals on demand). And what those young families offered in physical nourishment, the governing boards of the church offered in vocational nourishment. I was told, time and time again, that priority number one was my family. The work would be there, they assured me, and even though I was not about to neglect my job or calling, they knew that priorities needed to be elsewhere.

So for those lengthy cardiology appointments and for that yet-to-be-decided-upon surgery date, the church was amazingly supportive.

And I have seen this happen time and time again with people—not just the pastor—going through different life challenges. Hospitalizations, cancer treatments, family deaths, you name it, in my book, the church is the only place in society today that can come together and act as the extended family that we all so desperately need to get us through in this life. It does take a village, and they are the meal-makers, the shoulders to cry on, the unexpected hugs, the moral and spiritual support to keep the wheels of life moving. And that's not denominationally unique. That's something I have seen happen in churches of all shapes and sizes, of all theological leanings, of all socioeconomic make-ups.

So this isn't an evangelistic pitch, and yet it is—minus the bloody Jesus cartoons others will want to hand you on the street (don't take them, and if you do, find some hand sanitizer when you're done). If there's something or someone missing in your life, find that white steeple on the green or converted shopping mall gathering in your community. It's bound to have just what you're looking for—a place that you'll need, even though you don't know it yet.

And if that one church, perchance, doesn't welcome you—with all your differing abilities—with open arms, do yourself a favor and keep looking.

MAY 12, 2008

So a brief update for you all today. Did you notice the picture on the main page? Well, there's no more feeding tube! Yeah! Well, sort of…

We saw the feeding team last week. They told us to eliminate the 3 a.m. feed (thank God!) and then said that Jacob was doing so well with his feeds by mouth that they would consider taking the feeding tube out soon. (They actually said, given what they had read about him on paper, that they couldn't believe he was the same kid!) Anyway, with the feeding tube, Jacob had some other ideas. Saturday night he decided that he had had enough and yanked the tube out himself! So we've decided not to rush to put it back in (since he hasn't been using it much anyway). So now we have tubeless baby photos! Yeah!

As for what's next, it looks like the cardiac catheterization is going to happen. Probably in the beginning of June. Then, they're saying, that Jacob will have his surgery at around 5 months (so in August, we think).

So Jacob is doing well and he continues to get bigger. He's 7 pounds, 2 ounces now and sleeping well despite having three shots earlier today (normal baby vaccinations, don't worry)! As always, thanks for your prayers. Until next time…

JUNE 16, 2008

So we've been a bit neglectful in updating this page. We told you that would happen. Life has been busy, and we've just been working to make life at home as smooth for Noah and Jacob as it can be. And so far it seems to be working! (Imagine that!) Noah loves his little brother. He loves to spend time with him, sing to him, and kiss him goodnight.

As for Jacob, he's holding his own. He's going to have a cardiac catheterization sometime very soon (we're waiting to hear from the doctors as to when that might be). This is simply an overnight in the hospital as they get a very good picture of his heart in preparation for surgery. The surgery will likely be in July or August, and we're told that it will require Jacob to be in the hospital for about a week. Not too bad. We were thinking it might be worse.

Jacob's feeding tube is long gone. He's eating very well, smiling, cooing, making friends with Wally the Green Monster (take a look at the pictures), and starting to grab for Kristen's hair. We haven't had him officially weighed in a couple of weeks, but we assume he's up over 8 pounds now.

To tide you over, we've included a couple of pictures for you. We'll update you as soon as we know when things start happening. Thanks, as always, for your prayers. Until next time...

JUNE 30, 2008

So not too bad, only two weeks since our last update! Well, we finally have some news to share. We heard from Jacob's cardiologist, and Jacob will be heading to Boston on August 22nd for his cardiac catheterization. (Actually, he'll head in for a few hours of pre-op on the 21st.) Then he'll get to go home, before going in on the 22nd for the procedure. He should only be in the hospital one night, they tell us. While he's there they'll also do a 3-D echocardiogram. The two tests should give them a very good picture of his heart. This will enable them to have a pretty good idea of what's going to happen when he goes in for surgery.

Since he's doing so well, they now think that surgery will happen in the middle of September—when Jacob is about 6 months old. Again, they're not entirely sure of what the surgery will entail. They'll get some information from the procedure on the 22nd, and then they'll figure out exactly what they're going to do when the operation takes place. I guess that's somewhat standard practice, since they can't tell exactly what they're dealing with until they start the surgery.

So that's the news from here. Jacob last weighed in at 9 pounds 7 ounces. That's still tiny, but double what he was at birth! He continues to sleep well, eat well, and be his brother's favorite person in the world. He loves to talk to Wally the Green Monster and Mickey Mouse (yes, the stuffed animals). He'll have ten minutes, or so, of conversation with them and then start getting angry with them because they don't talk back! He's also taken to smiling quite a bit and making all sorts of new noises—all good developmental signs! As we keep telling everyone, right now he's just a normal baby—and we can't remember what life was like before he arrived! He's such a joy to have around!

Once again, thank you for all the love, support, and prayers. If anything changes we'll let you know. Be sure to check out the photo gallery—there are a couple new pictures in there. Until next time...

I realize that I haven't said a whole lot about Down syndrome itself, and while volumes have been written on this subject, a few words are in order. Aside from his heart procedures, echocardiograms, and feeding tubes—which is a lot—Jacob's life story reads like a typically developing child's life might read. He hits all of the developmental milestones, just a bit slower than some other kids might—and perhaps that's as good a definition as any of what Down syndrome is.[16]

Down syndrome occurs when a person is born with three, rather than two, copies of the twenty-first chromosome. (Humorously, I've seen T-shirts saying "I'm rocking my extra chromosomes," "My child has more chromosomes than your honors student!" and "My extra chromosome makes me extra cute.") This error in cell division is called nondisjunction. The extra chromosome is then replicated in every cell in the body. This accounts for 95 percent of all Down syndrome cases, the medical name for which is Trisomy 21 (the other two types of Down syndrome are mosaicism and translocation). The chromosomal (that's how the word is properly spelled) difference alters the course of development for people with Down syndrome. Yet even though they share this common chromosomal difference, it should be stressed that each person with Down syndrome is very definitely a unique child of God.

First discovered by John Langdon Down, an English physician, in 1866, Down syndrome is the most commonly occurring chromosomal condition (though there are many others), with one in every 691 babies being born with Down syndrome. Although mothers are at an increased risk of having a baby with Down syndrome as they get older, babies with Down syndrome are born to mothers of all ages, races, ethnicities, and socioeconomic statuses. In fact, 80 percent of Down syndrome babies (like Jacob) are born to mothers under the age of thirty-five. Today more than 400,000 people are living with Down syndrome in the United States alone.

Common traits of people with Down syndrome are low muscle tone, small stature, an upward slant to the eyes, and a single deep crease across the center of the palm. Medical challenges (like heart conditions, intestinal problems, eye problems, and hearing problems) commonly affect people with Down syndrome, and all people with Down syndrome experience some form of cognitive delay, though the effect is usually moderate to mild. Life expectancy of people with Down syndrome has risen from twenty-five years in 1983 to sixty today—due in large part to medical advances and a better understanding of Down syndrome.

Yet neither medical conditions nor cognitive challenges prevent people with Down syndrome from going to mainstream schools, holding down jobs, living independently, forming relationships, getting married, and functioning as contributing members of society.

So, *genetically*, that's who Jacob is. But to us he's just Jacob. Music-loving, smile-that-can-light-up-a-church-bearing, laugh-that-can-set-a-whole-room-into-hysterics-boasting, Jacob. And as such, we choose to view him as we believe God views him. For even though "society… [has] labeled people either "able" or "disabled,"" as Webb-Mitchell points out, "God has a different idea of the human condition."[17] In God's eyes we are all just God's children—uniquely made, uniquely loved, uniquely granted God's grace no matter what our ability level. Down syndrome just makes Jacob who he, uniquely, is—and that's just the way God loves him: as a person, not as a disability.

Not to mention that's the way we love him too.

JULY 15, 2008

So, as many of you know, we had Jacob's baptism on Sunday. (We want to wish a very, very special thank you to our good friends Rev. Brad Hirst and Rev. Beth Hoffman for making the service perfect!) Jacob behaved beautifully throughout the entire service, except when Brad decided to put some of that holy water on his head. He then let the congregation know that he has quite a set of lungs on him! Apparently that was the Holy Spirit moving and letting us know that it is alive and well in Jacob! That's good news indeed! We capped off the day with a very enjoyable cookout with our family and friends.

Now for some health news… A woman from Early Intervention (a program to aid the development of children with Down syndrome and other disabilities) came by today. She said that Jacob's "social skills"(the way he responds to people) were within the typically developing range; he has a mild delay in "cognitive communication and self-help skills"—basically, the reason for this delay is that he says mostly vowel sounds and not consonant sounds, and he's still on formula and not solid foods yet (though this will likely be changing very soon); and he has a significant delay in "gross motor and fine motor skills"—this is likely a combination of the heart problem and the Down syndrome, Jacob will receive therapy in this area once he has his surgery (to do so now would likely tire him out too much so that he wouldn't eat well—and getting bigger is his most important job right now!).

So those are the nuts and bolts as to where Jacob stands. He has also had some slight hearing issues (these are likely due to a build-up of fluid in his ears, but he will be getting checked again soon for this as well).

As far as weight goes, he was weighed on Monday, and he came in at 10 pounds on the nose and 23 inches long. This is slightly behind average, but given where he started, we're ok with where he is!

So that's it for this update. August 22 is the cardiac catheterization, and the surgery is still going to be sometime in September. We appreciate all the prayers (keep 'em going), and will keep posting as we get more news. Be sure to check out the photos—there are some great new ones in there. Until next time...

It is a sad state of affairs that people have been barred from participating in the sacraments because it is perceived that they do not fully understand them. As a child, I remember attending a worship service with my youth group at another church and being told that we could not take communion until we were older. The perception was, clearly, that we just didn't "get it" enough to partake. I was hurt, watching others share the bread and cup right in front of my eyes. The sacrament was close enough to touch and smell, but too far off for me to taste that day—just as it is on any given Sunday for those of differing abilities who are similarly denied access. This is a tragedy and a travesty in my view. For to bar those with differing abilities—or anyone for that matter—from the free gifts of grace, love, and blessing that the sacraments make tangible is to suggest that one has to "understand" a sacrament before one can take part in it. Understand a sacrament? Really? That's to say that the people in the pews understand, completely, what happens when bread is broken and blessed or water is poured. I don't think so.

There is mystery to be found in the sacraments—that's what makes them so powerful. If we understood all that they stood for, that would rob them of their power—as a bit of that mystery, mingled with the Holy Spirit, can make for a pretty profound experience. Thus, to bar a certain group of people from receiving the sacraments because they don't understand is something that I just can't wrap my mind around.

Blessedly our congregation was not only willing, but eager to allow those sacramental waters of baptism to be poured, God's love to be showered, and the support of all those witnessing to be doused all over Jacob. Even though there was an even bigger blessing of belonging and acceptance to come (though we're not there yet!), on this day baptism did exactly what it should—it overwhelmed us with the blessing of God's love and grace.

In my friend and colleague Brad's arms, Jacob was baptized like Noah, like countless others I have baptized, and like the thousands who have felt the water leave the eighteenth-century baptismal bowl we use, to be poured, showered, sprinkled, and doused on their foreheads—a special blessing from God with a dual purpose. First, the act is a formal welcome of the child into the church, as the congregation promises their love, support, and care to the one baptized. In other words, they promise to keep doing what they'd been doing all along. And second, while I personally have an issue with the idea that baptism "cleanses" a child of sin (after all, what sins could a four-month-old have committed?), the baptismal blessing from God signals a new beginning. As *The Unofficial Handbook of the United Church of Christ* so eloquently states: "Baptism is a one-time-only bath supercharged with God's Spirit. The baptized will get dirty again, but by God's grace, the dirt won't stick."[18] And it is during that bath that God's formal welcome and acceptance of a child—newly blessed *because of* who he or she was uniquely created to be—is celebrated.

As any parent can attest, that blessing and acceptance means a lot. As the parents of a child with differing abilities, I'd say that they mean just a bit more. For they mark the acceptance, inclusion, and affirmation that will not always be granted to the child who is dripping wet from those baptismal waters. And if the church cannot be the place in which such acceptance happens—no matter who you are or where you are on life's journey, as we say in the UCC—then we, as people of faith, need to seriously rethink who we are and how we are *pretending* to be the church, acting as God's hands and feet on earth.

Mercifully on that day we weren't pretending. We were being the church. And our *screaming* wet child made sure we heard his approval.

JULY 31, 2008

Well… not much of an update today (we really just wanted to post a few new photos!). So we'll just give you a brief update. Jacob is somewhere between 10 pounds, 9 ounces and 10 pounds, 12 ounces (depending on whose scale you believe). He's fighting some congestion (and getting nebulizer treatments for it), in hopes he can have it beat in time for the catheterization—as they won't do the procedure if he's congested. Other than that, it's life as it has been—getting bigger and waiting for surgery in September. Thanks for the continued prayers. Until next time…

AUGUST 22, 2008

Catheterization was a success![21]

Hi everyone… well, it's been a long couple of days in the hospital, but Jacob came through his cardiac catheterization very well. He's resting in his room with us now (and still somewhat dazed and cranky, waiting for food), but all in all things went well.

We came in yesterday for the pre-op procedures. He had a chest X-ray, echocardiogram, EKG, and a bunch of other tests with acronyms that I can't remember. This included a feeding test done just to make sure all the gastrointestinal pieces were working—and that came out fine. While here, however, they noticed that Jacob's red blood cell count was high (this happens in children who do not have great oxygen saturation). So, with the red blood cell count high and him still being a little guy, they decided to keep him last night. So Mom got to stay in with the little guy and pretty much get no sleep. Dad got to go back to Mimi and Grampy's house to play with Noah for a while (and go for a late night run).

This morning started early. Jacob went in for his catheterization. It was about a four-hour procedure. They were able to get some pictures of his heart, measure where the blood was going, look at blood pressure in the lungs, and a bunch of other things. Sometimes they have to do some work other than just look around (like opening up blood vessels that are too small), but they didn't have to do any of that. That's good. They did notice that one loop of Jacob's intestines was a little high up. They do not think this is a major problem, but will remedy it during his surgery if it looks like it needs fixing.

After a few hours in recovery, we're now back in Jacob's room waiting to get him some real food (he's been about 21 hours without anything but sugar water, so you can imagine how happy he is!). They'll continue to monitor his vital stats. They have mentioned that he might not have to spend the night tonight, but we think that's highly unlikely. We think he'll be here until Saturday (and Mom is all revved up for another night on the fold-out chair!).

As for going forward, the cardiologist will meet with the surgeon on Monday and read the results of the catheterization. This will help them decide what surgery to do. They think that they'll get us a surgery date within the next week. They said that they will likely go into the surgery with a couple of options on the table— and then see how Jacob responds to what they're doing as they start fixing him up, and let that tell them which way to go. (While this means that we won't know what the surgery will look like, we actually find this comforting—better to have multiple options than just one!)

So that's about it from Boston. Jacob will be home tomorrow at the latest. We're looking forward to putting this step behind us, and moving on toward the surgery. Thank you for all the prayers and well wishes—we really appreciate them. We'll keep you posted on anything else that happens. Until next time...

Back to the hallowed grounds of Children's Hospital, and I don't use those words lightly. Although I believe that God can be encountered anytime, anywhere, by anyone (especially since I believe a piece of God resides in each one of us), I believe that there are places in this world that are examples of sacred space. Celtic Christians call these "thin places"—the spaces in which the realm of God and the realm of humanity come so close to touching, that the barrier separating them is that of a translucent veneer. Theologian and author Marcus Borg puts it beautifully: "Thin places are places where the veil momentarily lifts, and we behold God, experience the one in whom we live, all around us and within us."[20] Boston Children's Hospital is, for me, one such place.

It's one of those places where goose bumps appear on my skin, inexplicably, when I walk through those revolving doors. It's a place where the cafeteria food takes on a sacramental quality. And it's a space where the hands of the doctors look and the words of the nurses sound as if they are Jesus's.

As such, when we went in for this cardiac catheterization, I knew we were entering into holy, hallowed ground. This was so much the case, that after Jacob's procedure ended, and they were talking about sending him home late that afternoon, we resisted. I know that the staff was somewhat perplexed by this, since most people can't wait to get out of the hospital, but we felt that Jacob needed a bit more time before heading home—and that's what he got. He got an extra night in a place where miracles have been—and would soon be for him—performed.

And so it is to that chapter in this story that we must turn now. A chapter in which sacred space could not begin to describe where we would be walking, talking, crying, and praying.

Come, for all things are now ready for surgery number two.

SEPTEMBER 4, 2008

Surgery Date is Set

Hi everyone, just a short note tonight. We have finally received a surgery date from Boston Children's Hospital. Jacob will be going in on October 15th. Much like his catheterization, he'll be in on October 14th for some pre-op work. Then he'll come home (we hope!), before going in for surgery on the 15th. Again, we don't know what the surgery will entail, exactly, as they're still working out those details (and likely won't know until they actually start the surgery). Jacob could be in the hospital anywhere from 4–14 days. Since his surgery is more on the complex side, they tend to think it'll be on the longer end. He'll initially spend some time in the Cardiac ICU and then transfer to the regular cardiac floor after that. Just how long all that takes, we can't say for sure.

So that's about all. Jacob had an appointment with his cardiologist today and he's doing very well post-catheterization. We are just relived that we can now begin to arrange our lives around his surgery. We'll certainly keep you posted if anything changes, and, of course, we'll keep you up to date once everything gets underway.

As always, thanks for your thoughts and prayers. Until next time…

SEPTEMBER 22, 2008

So what is this surgery all about?

Hello everyone! Since we have set Jacob's surgery date, everyone keeps asking us what the surgery is all about. So, I thought we'd take some time and explain what we know. I realize this might be a recap for some of you, but please bear with me...

Jacob was born with three working heart chambers and one that was malformed (and not working particularly well). His body has since adjusted to living with three chambers— forming valves in incorrect places, and allowing for oxygenated and nonoxygenated blood to mix freely. This is why Jacob's oxygen saturation level changes so much. Sometimes he gets plenty of oxygen; sometimes he struggles. The good news is that he's not blue (which they told us he would be). The bad news is that he cannot stay like this forever—he needs to have his heart repaired.

So, the plan is to go in and fix that fourth chamber. Ideally they will rebuild that chamber, fix the valves, and correct the blood flow. This will leave Jacob with a normal heart and will be the most ideal for long-term health and success. This is what they're planning to do. However, they admit that a lot of this is guess work. They need to get inside Jacob's heart and see how he does as they begin fixing things. So, should that not work, there is a back-up plan.

Apparently (and here's where my ignorance with anatomy shines through), there is a way that they can "create" a fourth chamber. This would be a place for the blood to collect and then be rerouted to the body that bypasses that malformed fourth chamber. If that doesn't work, I believe there is a third option. This one, however, as I understand it, would require Jacob to have multiple surgeries over the course of a couple of years.

So that's basically what we know. Jacob will go in to surgery with a plan, but we won't know if they can execute that plan until

83

after surgery. So we'll go in with fingers crossed and hope for the best. Again, the more they can keep his heart functioning "normal," the better for long-term health. As our cardiologist said to us, with a successful repair Jacob will do all the things a normal kid will do, he just won't be an Olympic athlete (but then, who among us is?). The Special Olympics, however, is another story altogether. I'm already measuring Jacob for his sweat suit to wear on the medal stand :).

So that's the surgery news. As for the rest of life, Jacob is doing well. He was 12 pounds, 12 ounces at his last weigh-in. He continues to eat well. He has a mighty grip, smiles and babbles beautifully, and yesterday he rolled over for the first time! (You had to be there to hear Noah... "Come on buddy, I know you can do it, just a little more buddy!" So cute.) Noah is in preschool and loving every minute of it. We're just hoping that he doesn't bring anything home to "share" with Jacob. Jacob has been more congested recently, so we're just hoping that it's allergies, or nothing too serious to derail surgery plans.

That's enough for now. October 15th is the date (pre-op on October 14th). Which reminds me, we met some friends in the hospital whose daughter is going in for her heart surgery this week. So please keep Luna and her family in your prayers along with Jacob.

It goes without saying, but we sincerely appreciate your love and support. Until next time...

But before the surgery a quick detour to Emmaus. After all, we know well now that detours are just part of the journey. So to Emmaus we go. And before you ask, it isn't (though it probably should be) a city in Holland.

Coincidence, happenstance, or the movement of the Holy Spirit in our midst? As you can probably guess, the latter of these is my preferred way of describing those moments of serendipity that come into our lives from time to time. One such moment occurred as we were riding the elevators in Children's Hospital and met Luna's parents. It's a story that I recounted as part of the first sermon I preached after Jacob's birth and first surgery:

"Probably about three or four days after Jacob's surgery, when he was about a week old, Kristen and I were in Children's Hospital, heading downstairs on the elevator to get something for lunch. Now, in case you've

never been in Children's Hospital, parents are required to wear name badges that say what unit their child is staying in. And so it was that we entered the elevator—badges and all—only to notice another couple in the elevator with similar badges saying "8 South"—Children's Cardiac ICU.

As the doors closed we all stared at the numbers above our heads, not making eye contact—as people so often do in elevators. It was then that the woman said something to us. She said that she had noticed our badges and asked us to tell her what we were there for. Touched by this question, we shared Jacob's story with them. Upon finishing we asked them what brought them to Children's. And to our amazement, as they began to share their story, it was remarkably similar to ours.

Their daughter had been born a day after Jacob. She had nearly the same cardiac diagnosis. She had already had one surgery and was facing more in the months to come. Word for word, just about, their story was the story that we were living. Amazed by this, our conversation continued as we got off the elevator and headed down the hall to the cafeteria, with each of us sharing more and more about our experiences over the week passed.

Just before we reached the cafeteria, for curiosity sake, I decided to ask them where they lived. While I won't share exactly what they told us, all four of us were astonished to find out that they live in a community that neighbors us here in Kittery. Although we went our separate ways at lunchtime, we made a point of connecting with each other three or four more times throughout the week. We have since exchanged names, addresses, e-mails, and have already begun an online correspondence, with the hopes of getting together once all of us are a little less sleep deprived!

Needless to say, it was an eye-opening encounter for us. You might even say that it was our own Emmaus experience."

The story for that Sunday was the story of Emmaus—found in Luke 24:13–32. As the story goes, the disciples were distraught that Jesus had been crucified. As such, they were headed to a village called Emmaus—likely to resume their old lives, once again, since the Messiah had been killed. And it's on this journey that Jesus (although not immediately recognizable) encounters the disciples and asks them to tell him what has happened. Perplexed that this stranger doesn't know what has just transpired—since everyone in Jerusalem seems to—the disciples share their story.

When evening comes the disciples then invite Jesus to spend the night with them—first-century hospitality at its best. And it's after this, when Jesus breaks bread in their midst (the broken bread connecting with their broken spirits), that the disciples' eyes are opened and they recognize that their companion is none other than Jesus Christ. In the sharing of their story with Jesus—and of Jesus sharing his story with them—the interaction of the men and Jesus moved to a very profound place.

On that Sunday back in the pulpit I stood up there and suggested that we'd do well, as people of faith, to share our stories with one another. For it's in the sharing and the hearing of such stories, that we are often blessed to recognize the way that God is living and moving in our midst. That was certainly the case with our elevator encounter.

For in sharing Jacob's story, and in hearing our companions' story, we quickly moved from elevator acquaintances to friends (still to this day) whose common bond and life experience enabled us to walk part of this journey of life together. It's a bond that, I have no doubt, will continue for many years to come.

Living as a parent of a child with differing abilities, such bonds are essential. To be able to share common experiences, wrestle through common problems, and look into the eyes of another human being who knows what echocardiograms and breathing tubes are like, is amazing. The work that organizations such as the National Down Syndrome Congress, the National Down Syndrome Society and others do in this area is essential. For in those interactions, as we stand shoulder to shoulder and walk arm in arm with those who are traveling those same wilderness roads, I don't think it's too much of a stretch to say that on those roads we do, indeed, walk with Jesus.

And we all know that when you're in a deep, dark forest of trees, spotting such a companion can make all the difference in the world.

OCTOBER 14, 2008

And so the journey begins…

On Monday afternoon we made our way south from Maine to set up "base camp" (minus the Sherpas) at Kristen's parents' house. Then it was off to Boston just before 6 a.m. this morning. Jacob had blood work drawn, an EKG, chest X-rays, an abdominal ultrasound, and we had a whole bunch of consultations. All in all it amounted to a long day of waiting around.

The good news is that we have the green light for surgery tomorrow. We have to be in Boston at 7:30 a.m. sharp. Jacob is the first case of the day. The surgeon tells us that the surgery should last between 3 and 5 hours. So it promises to be a long morning. They are planning to go ahead with the most optimal surgery, which they are calling a "two-ventricle repair." This will leave Jacob with the most normal heart possible. If that doesn't work, they'll go for a "one and a half-ventricle repair." If that doesn't work, then we're looking at a shunt. I'm not sure of the details of all of these, but I do know that the shunt is not a particularly good situation for kids with Down syndrome (something to do with heart and lung pressures). So we'll be hoping for the two-ventricle or one and a half-ventricle repair. Again, it's a matter of getting in there, starting to fix things, and seeing how Jacob does. So it's kind of wait and see.

They told us that Jacob got a lot of attention at the morning case study. All the cardiologists working today (Children's Hospital has a total of 60 of them on staff) review every case, and Jacob got them talking quite a bit. They are calling him "unique," and the surgeon said that he has never done a repair exactly like Jacob's— he's done some like Jacob's, but not exactly the same. With that, he said he's very optimistic that we'll have a good outcome.

The only other piece of business was that Jacob's intestine appears to be high in his body. They did an ultrasound to see if that is truly the case (the results weren't in when we left). If it is, they might need to do a minor repair on that when they're in there (or possibly at a later date).

That's all we know. We're back at Kristen's parents, looking for a relaxing evening (and me getting out for a run!), and then forgetting about what's coming by watching the Red Sox pull even with Tampa Bay! Then it's off to bed for a loooong day tomorrow. We'll post as soon as we're able, but don't expect to hear until mid to late afternoon at the earliest.

We appreciate all the prayers and well wishes and hope to have some very good news for you when we post tomorrow. Until next time...

I didn't really understand the enormity of the words I wrote when they first made it on to the computer screen. Words like "lots of attention" from sixty of the best cardiologists in the world, "unique," and "not exactly the same," should have been clues for me. But they weren't. All I knew is that in a few short hours I would have to make the all-too-familiar walk down the long surgical corridor to give my seven-month-old baby a kiss goodbye underneath the bright, sterile operating room lights. Goodbye for a few hours, is what I thought; though it would be different goodbye than I had expected, as those days postsurgery moved on.

On that night it was about giving Noah and Jacob a bigger hug than usual when they went to bed. It was trying to find a comfortable spot on my in-laws' couch—a familiar resting place for me, by now. It was trying to pass the time with a Red Sox game that just couldn't hold my attention. It was attempting to catch a few hours of sleep, which had no chance of being caught. The image that kept flashing in my mind was that solitary cardiac ICU room, with a three-day-old Jacob in my arms, and tears filling my eyes as I dreamed dreams for the slumbering child who had so much ahead of him. All I could think about was whether those dreams—his dreams, my dreams, our dreams—were now in jeopardy.

I'm sure I prayed, but I don't know what I said; I probably didn't say anything. It was a Garden of Gethsemane moment for me. I knew what awaited in the morning. I knew it was going to be trying. I knew it was going to be painful. I would love for God to have dramatically changed the course of events we were about to undertake, but I knew that God's role was not to shelter us from the storms of life, but to help us navigate through. That night the seas couldn't have been more violent.

I'm sure Kristen and I talked on the ride into Boston—but what do two parents about to release their child for open heart surgery really say to each other? We had so many questions, so many fears, so many uncertainties in our minds that I can't honestly recall any of what happened that night and morning.

But what happened after would leave such an indelible mark on my soul that I never will forget.

OCTOBER 15, 2008

Surgery is a Success!

If you heard a collective (although guarded) sigh of relief coming from the Boston way around 2 p.m., I'm sure it was from us. Jacob's surgeon came out to talk with us and told us that Jacob is doing well. He was able to have the full two- ventricle repair (the most optimal outcome), and his valves are working better than they expected. However, the doctor did say that this was one of the most challenging surgeries he has ever had to do. (Mind you, he's one of the best surgeons in the world too.) So Jacob gave them quite a time, I guess. Apparently Jacob's malformed chamber was extremely small, which gave them very little to work with as they recreated that chamber. So he is right on the edge of a two-ventricle repair. This means that they will keep him very sedated for at least two days in ICU. This will be to watch how his heart adjusts to working in this new way. But all in all, it's good news. We'll just wait and see how he progresses and how he adjusts to having a normal heart. That will go a long way toward telling us how long he'll be in ICU and how long the hospital stay will be in total.

Right now Kristen and I are in the ICU waiting room. We haven't seen Jacob yet (it takes a while for them to transport him up and get him settled in his room). We're hoping to get in within 30 minutes or so. They tell us Jacob will be very puffy, blue, and that he will have many, many tubes and lines coming out of him. This will be very reminiscent of his first surgery back in March—breathing tube, chest tube, arterial line, etc. So he'll be that way for a couple of days, we assume, and then it'll be a process of taking things away from him little by little.

Kristen and I are exhausted, but doing well. It was a long day, watching other families come and go, as we waited and waited for news. We're happy this piece of the journey is over, and guardedly

optimistic that Jacob will do well with his newly formed heart and
hit his milestones in a timely fashion.

That's all we know for now. If there's more information to
share, I may post again tonight after we talk with the nurses, etc.
Otherwise, we'll check in again tomorrow. It was wonderful to be
supported by all of your love, prayers, and support—we could feel
it, believe me, way down here in Boston. In fact, that's what got us
through today. So thank you, once again, from the bottom of our
hearts, and we'll get more news to you (and maybe pictures too) as
soon as we can. Until next time…

We spent the morning in a bookstore. Can you believe that? A bookstore. Walking around, trying to pass the time, thinking that we might actually find something to read that could hold our attention. The attempt was futile. But we couldn't bear to be in that waiting room with another my-child-is-soon-to-be-tonsil-less, hysterical mother. This time I might not have been able to walk away. So we perused the bookstore. We grabbed some lunch and brought it back to the hospital. And we found some quiet chairs at the end of the hall where we wouldn't have to listen to, or talk to, anyone.

We simply traded glances with other parents, our hollow eyes saying the same thing back and forth to one another: "We understand."

I have a picture on my refrigerator of what I looked like when I crossed the finish line of the Boston Marathon (another story soon to be told). I think it's safe to say that Jacob's surgeon didn't look much better when we saw him post-surgery. I raised my right fist, slightly, in triumph that I had covered all 26.2 miles. Jacob's surgeon's chosen victory celebration was a sweeping off of his surgical cap and falling into a chair in one fell swoop. Victory. Exhausted victory.

We were all exhausted. Every staff person, doctor, or nurse who came down the hall had families sitting up at attention. When the doctor walked by us, and then the family next to us, to bring news to someone farther down the hall, the remaining families looked at one another exasperatedly, because we knew what each was feeling. I can only imagine what they were thinking when they saw this rugged, heavyset cardiac surgeon slump into the chair beside Kristen and me.

Difficult and demanding doesn't capture how tough a surgery this was. We were told that Jacob's heart was about the size of his wrist—at this point perhaps the size of a super ball. And our surgeon's job was to carve out—within that super ball-sized heart—a new chamber for blood to flow, and create valves where there were none before. I can't even begin to imagine what that must have been like—and I don't really want to imagine it. I'm just thankful that Jacob's heart was in the hands of one of the most skilled surgeons in the world—who was now seated, exhausted, in front of us. Our little Jacob was making a name for himself already.

Our little Jacob. When we saw him he didn't look like our little Jacob. Not as puffy and blue as we expected him to be, but with more lines and tubes coming in and out of him than we could have imagined. After being summoned to the ICU waiting room, the time spent there turned out to be hours, not minutes, as they got all the lines in place and made sure Jacob was resting where he needed to be.

The one thing we wanted to do was to race in, pick him up, see that infectious smile, and give him the biggest hug of his life. But that was not to be. Jacob could not be moved. He was medically paralyzed so that all the lines and tubes stayed in place. He didn't open his eyes. He didn't smile. He didn't acknowledge our voices, our touches, or our kisses. He simply lay there. And we simply watched. With tears in our eyes and a guarded relief in our hearts, we were transported back to those first few days of Jacob's life when he was close enough to touch but too far away to hold. Again we sat in that space. Down the hall from our first stint in the cardiac ICU, the bells and beeps, sterile smells and sights, all came racing back to us.

As did the familiar looks, glances, and smiles shared among parents as we passed one another in the hallway, understanding what each was going through, hoping and praying that each of our stays would be quick and uneventful.

Ours would be neither.

OCTOBER 16, 2008

Day Two...Going Strong...

It was an uneventful night for Jacob. In the hospital that's very good news. Jacob had a little fever yesterday afternoon (not unexpected post heart surgery), but that has come down. Now they continue to play with medicines—go up on this, go down on that, etc.—trying to keep his blood pressure in an optimal spot. It's really like solving a jigsaw puzzle that keeps changing by the minute. We have so much respect for the doctors and nurses who have been able to navigate such a confusing road! They have been amazing and have treated us incredibly well. Let's put it this way—in the ICU Jacob has his own nurse who literally works nonstop for twelve hours—there's that much tweaking going on.

Jacob continues to stay sedated today. They are watching the pressures in his heart continue to even themselves out. This process is aided, not surprisingly, when he's not moving. The plan is to reduce sedation tomorrow and then see how he does. If all goes well, they will work to get the breathing tube out tomorrow or Saturday. From there, we are told, things progress pretty quickly. So hopefully not too long after that, we might move out of cardiac ICU and onto the regular cardiac inpatient floor. But all in due time.

We met with Jacob's cardiologist, surgeon, nurse practitioner, and anesthesiologist this morning. They are all amazed at how well he's doing. They're using phrases like "perfect" and "right where we want him to be"—so that is good to hear. Interestingly, they told us that ten years ago they never would have even tried this surgery on Jacob. They would have gone for a 2 step procedure (which, if things do not go well, is still a fallback option for Jacob). However, in people with Down syndrome, they have found that the two-ventricle repair is much better for their long-term health. So they pushed the envelope a little, to see if Jacob would handle the more optimal repair—and so far he seems to be. If all goes well, he will likely be a case that they will point to, in the future, for evidence of going for the two-ventricle repair in other children.

We are all doing well and trying to take care of ourselves (as best as we can on cafeteria food). Noah is in the very loving (and very apt to spoil) hands of my parents, Kristen's parents, and Kristen's sister, Traci. He's having fun with his extended Massachusetts sleepover as Jacob goes into the hospital to have "a boo boo in his heart fixed." Kristen stayed in the ICU last night, while I went to Kristen's parents to see Noah for a bit. Assuming all continues to go well, we're both planning to go back to Kristen's parents' house tonight. (While he's sedated, there's not much for us to do in the evenings anyway.)

So I think that's all for now. We are humbled by the many, many messages that you have posted on the page, and even more so by the countless prayers that have been offered on Jacob's behalf. You know he's a pretty special guy when one of the anesthesiologists comes in and tells us that she was praying for him last night too. As we continue to say, Children's Hospital is a very special place because of the amazing people who work here. We are truly blessed to have such an amazing medical facility close by.

We'll continue to try and give you daily updates while Jacob is in the hospital. We'll work on getting some pictures too, but right now he's not particularly photogenic (none of us would be with 11+ medicines, two chest tubes, a catheter, breathing tube, and various other things sticking out of us!). But soon those will be removed and we'll have a smiling baby, with a brand new heart, to show you. Until next time...

Prayer. It's a funny thing really. I say it to parishioners all the time: "I'll be praying for you." We throw it around in many and varied forms on Sunday mornings and we invite people to lift up prayers of joy and concern so that we, as a congregation, can hold them together. But what does that really mean, to pray?

Well, for me, prayers do not have to be in words, though they can be; they do not have to be in silence, though they can be that too; they certainly don't have to be well thought out and articulated; they don't even have to be understood by the person doing the praying (in fact, sometimes I think the best aren't). Prayer, really, is a state of mind. It is, as the Jewish author Abraham Joshua Heschel writes: "an invitation to God to intervene in our lives...the opening of a window to [God] in our will."[21] In this way, it is a state of being in relationship with God—of opening oneself to hear—as we say in the United Church of Christ, how God might be speaking—even as we enable God to "hear" the words we say, and the words we don't say, that arise from the longings of our hearts. It's that time when we pause, in some way, to recognize the presence of the God who is with us always.

Sometimes we do that with ourselves in mind. Sometimes we do that with others in mind. But I know God knows what we're bringing to those moments, even before we know (that is, assuming we ever really know). And the fact of the matter is, I think that God will love and care for the person we're praying for (ourselves or someone else), regardless of whether we hold that person in prayer or not. But still, prayer does something. It does something to God; otherwise, why would we pray? It does something to the one being prayed for and the one doing the praying. I'd heard members of our church testify to that time and time before, saying prayer is what pulled them through a tough time. This was the first time that I was able to really be on the receiving end, and it confirmed for me what I knew already in my heart—they were right.

So it seems to me that in some divine way—utilizing the Spirit of God that is within and all around us—God must channel all of that energy that is lifted up in prayer for a person to that person. So not only are you feeling God's love, when someone prays for you, you are feeling their love (which is really a reflection of God's love) wrapped up in more of God's love. Is it any wonder that you can feel it? And it helps. In a palpable way. Prayer is God's way of giving exactly what a person needs.

Which is to say that when I pray, I'm not presumptuous enough to claim to know what it is that the person I'm praying for needs. Only God truly knows that. So I don't pray for miracles to happen. I don't pray for someone to get better. I don't pray for specific outcomes, because my prayer may not be what the best outcome is. Instead, I pray for God's unmistakable presence and for the strength to get through situations—regardless of what may transpire in them.

So perhaps the anesthesiologist and others were praying for a miracle as Jacob recovered, I don't know. I just know I wasn't. I was merely praying for the strength to get through—the strength to handle seeing my baby hooked up to more wires than my brother's high-definition television, the strength to put one foot in front of the other, the strength to be exactly what I needed to be: not the strong and steady pastor who must anchor the most tumultuous situations, but simply Jacob's Dad. I wasn't praying for a miracle; I was praying for strength.

Turns out we needed both.

OCTOBER 17, 2008

Day Three...More Progress...

Well, it has been another positive day for Jacob in the Cardiac ICU. This morning he had the larger of his two chest tubes pulled, and this afternoon they have begun to take him off the paralytic. This enables him to move around a little. He has opened his eyes a few times and even grabbed on to Dad's finger. (Believe me, that's a great feeling, when you haven't felt it in a while!) The good news is that his temperature has stabilized (he was fluctuating quite a bit), and his heart rate and blood pressure continue to level themselves out. As he gets to move around more, the fluid he has built up in his system will be released (i.e., peed out), and this should help get the blood pressure and heart rate even more stable. But, so far so good. He is peeing a lot—which is a very good sign—and all in all people seem to be happy with the way things are going. While they haven't said, I would optimistically like to see him out of ICU on Sunday or Monday, but we'll wait and see.

We received a couple of nice gifts today. A Vermont teddy bear of Patch Adams arrived this morning (you know who you are... thank you!) and a South Shore Down syndrome group came by with a wonderful little care package for us. They just did a "Buddy Walk" last weekend, and some of the money raised goes to purchase gift packages for families in the hospital. For those of you who have spent an extended period of time in a hospital, you know those gift packages are a wonderful treat. So those two pick-me-ups were great to receive this morning—as are all of your comments. We love to read them, and we truly appreciate being in so many people's thoughts and prayers.

So not much else to say today. We'll continue to watch how he does without the paralytic. They seem to think he'll be pulling at his tubes very soon, so life should get interesting. And we can't wait until he tries to roll over! From there we just want to see things level out, and more tubes pulled. And hopefully we're on track to see that happen.

Again, thanks for the incredible love you have shown to us—it really comes through the webpage. We'll keep you posted and hope to have some more good news next time. And be sure to check out the pictures—there are a couple of pre-surgery photos there for you. Post-surgery are soon to follow! (And before I forget, we won't talk about the Revolution, but how 'bout those Red Sox... comebacks in 2004 and 2007, could it happen again??) Until next time...

If you've been in the hospital for an extended period of time before, you know that gifts can be a huge boon to an otherwise difficult, and frankly depressing, period of time. We received a couple that day. The first came in the form of a visit from members of a Massachusetts Down syndrome group. Affiliated with the Massachusetts Down Syndrome Congress, this is a group that organizes the Buddy Walk each year—in our case, a beautiful walk around Lake Quannapowit in Wakefield, Massachusetts. This brings together thousands of people with Down syndrome, their families, and their friends for an amazing afternoon and experience. Funds raised that day go to help increase Down syndrome awareness, advocate for Down syndrome rights, organize gatherings and events for the Down syndrome community, and, apparently, bring gifts to people in the hospital. This was our first taste of being a part of the "Down syndrome community." We met two parents who had stood by similar ICU beds and watched their own children heal. They visited, they talked, and they gave us moral support. We needed all that they had to give (which included gift cards for coffee and dinner and a few other "perks"). We vowed that day to make a difference in the Down syndrome community by participating in the Buddy Walk—which we have done every year since.

We also received a teddy bear. We still don't know who it came from. But it brought a smile to our faces, and it will bring some good memories to Jacob when he's old enough to see the bear, ask where it came from, and hear the story for himself. This was all in addition to a care package that a good friend gave us to take with us. With the number of their son's hospitalizations making it look like Jacob was a perfectly healthy child, they knew what we'd need. And their care package meant as much for what was in it—fan included—as it meant by what it said: "We've been in your shoes, we know what it's like, and we're with you on this journey 100 percent." Each gift was different. Each gift was incredibly meaningful in its own way.

As were the gifts of presence. Yes, *presence*, not presents. The chaplain who stopped by to talk. The family and friends who diligently visited, left messages on our CarePage, and were there to pick up the other end of the phone when needed to hear a voice. Those gifts were love—tangibly and intangibly sent our way—and we would never have made it through those first couple of postsurgery days without them.

This, without even knowing what lie ahead.

OCTOBER 18, 2008

A Couple of Steps Back

Well, after a few days of positive progress, I guess that some setbacks were to be expected. Shortly after I posted yesterday, Jacob began to have trouble keeping up his blood pressure and keeping down his heart rate. His heart hadn't been beating in rhythm (normal after heart surgery), so apparently that wasn't helping. Their solution has been to put Jacob back on the paralytic and to keep him quite cool. This is how he has done the best. They have also begun to pace his heart. This will take the burden off of him having to pump on his own, and hopefully help get his heart back into rhythm. It's not a major setback, but a setback nonetheless. The hard part for us is that we no longer get to look into Jacob's eyes or feel him grab our fingers. He's medically paralyzed again (and will be until we hear otherwise), and that's a hard state to see your child in for an extended period of time.

Things are quiet here on the weekends, so we don't know exactly what the plan is for today. Right now they are warming Jacob up a bit, and watching to see if that affects his heart rate or blood pressure. So far so good this morning. They are also continuing to give him diuretics to enable him to release excess fluid. Apparently, one of their theories is that if he can lose more fluid, then the heart will be less swollen and that will mean less stress on him and will help get things back on track. But again, it's a theory. A lot of this, we have learned, is educated guesswork and seeing how Jacob responds as they do this and remove that. So we'll hope that their tweaking today yields some positive results.

So that's about all from here. I'd be lying if I said that the setback hasn't frustrated Kristen and me. Jacob was going along well, so we weren't expecting what happened (even though, they say, it's not uncommon). It looks like we'll be in ICU longer than we had

*expected, and that's not a fun place to be. So we're hanging in there
and trying to keep a positive attitude. We appreciate all the time you
spend checking in here and all your love, prayers, and support. We
hope to have some better news to share the next time we post. Until
next time...*

PS—Go Sox!

We were now novice cardiac ICU nurses. We knew what all the
lines on the monitor above Jacob's head meant. We understood
heart rate, pulse oxygen level, breathing rate, and oxygen saturation.
We knew that an arterial line in Jacob gave a better blood pressure
reading than one taken externally with an inflatable cuff. And we knew
that adjustments to the paralytic medicine would affect each of these
numbers. And we knew what to look for and what to look out for. I
was particularly obsessed.

The nurse would come in, tweak this medicine or that, check this
line or that line, consult with the doctors, make a minor shift here and
there. And I watched each move like a hawk—one eye on the nurse and
the other on the monitor to see what numbers were changing. In fact,
I was so bad that at one point the nurse looked at me and said: "You
need to stop watching those numbers; you're going to drive yourself
crazy. That's my job. You just be the Dad."

The problem was, I was being the Dad. And with Jacob
unresponsive on the bed beneath me, the best Dad I thought I could
be was one who watched those numbers. And so I kept watching. And
I'm sure the nurse saw me simply as one of the thousands of Dads
she'd seen standing where I was standing, doing the exact same thing:
trying to be the best Dad we could be, when being the best Dad we
could be meant doing nothing. Absolutely nothing.

I haven't said much about the nursing staff. They were
absolutely amazing. Words can't convey how dedicated, talented, and
compassionate they were. I tried to thank them as much as I could
(I'm a stickler for saying "thank you"), but I know I didn't thank them
enough. And I won't even begin to try to describe them any further.
Knowing that words are futile I'll simply say that they were *amazing*
and leave it at that.

We also became very familiar with them. In fact, this is one thing
(of many) that Children's does masterfully—they try and keep nurses
paired up with the same patients as much as they are able. This is so

that the nurses can get to "know" patients—what they like and don't like, what works and doesn't work—in ways that can't be conveyed on charts and in computer notes.

We were blessed with one nurse, in particular, who turned out to be nothing short of *miraculous*.

OCTOBER 19, 2008.

Prayers Please!

Brace yourselves—today's post isn't a good one. Let me first just say that Jacob is ok. He's stable in ICU as I type. However, it has been quite a morning for him and us. While driving in this morning we received a call from the ICU. They had been taking the paralytic off of Jacob this morning, and his blood pressure fell, hard. He went into cardiac arrest. The ICU team responded right away, performed CPR, and got everything running again. (Have I said before how amazing these people are?) They literally saved Jacob's life this morning—and yet it's all in a day's work for them.

So as I said, Jacob is ok now. They believe that—and this is going to sound strange—that his heart is actually working too well. He has functioned for so long on poorly oxygenated blood going to his lungs, that now that things are pumping well, his body couldn't handle all the pressure in his lungs. That's what caused the cardiac arrest. So the plan is to keep him on the paralytic again today. They have installed a new lead into his body that measures pressure in his lungs. Tomorrow they will try to take him off the paralytic (with a SWAT team around him, I imagine). If his lung pressure goes up, then they will stop and give him some medicine (Viagra actually, and yes, that did make us all laugh this morning), which will reduce the pressure in his lungs. So hopefully that will get things moving again.

As for the heart attack, they don't believe that it caused any permanent damage. They will do an ultrasound on his head, but they're quite confident that it caused no harm to Jacob (the verdict on Mom and Dad, however, is still out).

The good news in all of this—and there actually is some— is that when they did an echocardiogram the surgeon said that he could not imagine the repair looking any better. So it was not heart failure that caused the cardiac arrest. In fact, they think that the malformed chamber in his heart has grown a bit—which is what they were hoping they would see. And the heart is pumping well. In fact, as I said earlier, almost too well for Jacob's body to compensate with right now. That's what caused the problem this morning.

So once again, Jacob is ok. He's receiving some blood and platelets and resting now. Kristen and I are picking up the pieces of ourselves that fell off as we were racing in here this morning, but we're also managing ok. Needless to say, we would appreciate your continued prayers for Jacob, us, and the incredible people taking care of him. Again, how do you say thank you to someone who saved your child's life? Words seem so futile. If you've got any suggestions, I'm all ears. Until next time…

P.S.—Go Sox again—we need them to keep playing so Jacob can watch them in the World Series!

As soon as I answered my cell phone Kristen started to drive faster. She didn't need me to say a word. She knew. And so did I when my phone rang early that Sunday morning. Too early. I'm not sure what I said, or if I said anything at all. The first words I heard when I answered the phone were: "This is the cardiac ICU. Let me assure you that Jacob is okay *now.*" Okay *now.* Translation: he wasn't okay before. I heard the words loud and clear—and I can picture exactly where I was when I heard them—rounding a sharp bend on Route 1 north in Chelsea.

It was that ICU-air-sucking Code Blue that we had heard too often before, only this time it sucked the air and life out of our car. Our room. Our boy. Code Blue. Heart attack. Our little boy nearly died on the table that very morning. As we broke speed limits—and nearly the sound barrier—to drive those remaining few miles, Kristen and I said little to each other. What words could be said? We comforted each other simply by being together, as we knew how to do so well by now. And I was thankful that she was the one driving—I'm not sure how I would have made it across the Charles River with a river flowing in my own eyes.

When we arrived in Boston we were not able to go in and immediately see Jacob—not that we could have held him anyway, though we still wanted to see our boy. Instead we had to wait in the cardiac ICU waiting room—an all-too-familiar place for us—until the doctor came out to talk to us and give us the all-clear. It was the very same man who had operated on Jacob a few days prior, and he looked equally as exhausted. Perhaps this was because he was called in early on a Sunday morning or perhaps from the intensity of the moment he just stood witness to. I'm not sure which, and we didn't ask.

As we listened to him with tears staining our faces, he made sure to explain, again, that Jacob was doing okay. He had been called in to do some surgery on Jacob to put a pulmonary line back in. With this in place they would have seen his lung pressure changing sooner than it did. But thanks to our nurse they saw it soon enough. Soon enough. Miraculous words.

"Jacob's nurse" as we came to call her, knew Jacob so well that even without that line in, she sensed something bad was happening. She knew Jacob didn't normally act the way he was acting (in other words, his numbers weren't doing what she was familiar with), and so she became concerned. In fact, she called the Code Blue before a code might normally have been called. And in so doing, she saved Jacob's life. That's not to say that he would have died if she didn't call it when she did (though he could have), but she made certain that any damage to Jacob or his heart would be as minimal as possible. That's nothing short of miraculous.

So what is a miracle then? Well, my definition isn't very stringent. It's when something happens on this earth that defies explanation. It's a sign that points to God. It's when something that couldn't have been wrought by human hands alone actually takes place through divinely aided human hands or simply divine hands. It's when something so extraordinary occurs that we just have to throw up our hands and say: "Wow!"

A rainbow touching down on the place where a tornado has wrought tremendous devastation; a young girl found alive underneath the rubble days after an earthquake hit; the extra weeks of life "given" to a dying woman after the medical professionals have said, "It'll be a matter of days now"; the birth of a child of differing abilities to a family who didn't know they needed him until they got him; the insight of a nurse whose intuition trumped the world's best technological equipment: miracles, all of them. Miracles. You've seen them—you just may not have known it. You've had them happen to you—you just may not have noticed.

A miracle happened that day. Actually, make that two. One happened in that ICU room. The other was that God granted us a miracle when we didn't know enough to pray for it.

Now why, we might ask, are some people blessed with miracles while others are not? I don't know. Add that to the list (yes, I'm working on one) of questions that I would love to have an opportunity to grill God about some day. I don't know why miracles happen some places and not others. Maybe they're actually happening in those other places too, and we just don't see them, or recognize them, or understand them. It's all about living into the mystery that is our faith—understanding that we cannot and will not understand it all. Author Frederick Buechner explains it well: "There are mysteries which you can solve by taking thought…There are other mysteries which do not conceal a truth to think your way to but whose truth is itself the mystery…To say that God is a mystery is to say that you can never nail [God] down. Even on Christ the nails proved ultimately ineffective."[22]

All that I know is that I don't know enough about miracles to pray for them to happen. Maybe others do know, and did pray. If so, thank you.

I'll just choose to keep on not understanding, and giving thanks to God that God is working, even—and especially— when I just can't seem to get it.

I don't remember what happened when we finally made it into Jacob's ICU room. I vaguely recall a lot of people in there and cleaning up the floor (they were less concerned with where needle wrappers fell than with Jacob's health, fortunately). And I know I made a joke (which wasn't a joke) that if I had been there for the Code Blue, then they would have had two patients on the floor. Another miracle? Maybe. But probably not. I'll simply choose to give thanks for the miracles that I know happened that day—even if I'll never understand why.

Hanging in There

First of all, let me just say thank you to you all for your tremendous support. Yesterday was rough, and it meant the world to us to be able to read all your kind words and to know that so many of you are thinking of us and keeping us in your prayers. Your hugs, love, and prayers are being felt miles away.

Well, it's been a little over 24 hours since the dust has settled from yesterday's events. The good news is that Jacob has remained stable since then. His blood pressure, heart rate, oxygen level, etc., all look good. So he's hanging in there, but still on the paralytic. We thought they might try to lift the paralytic today, but that's not the plan. They have noticed that Jacob has some congestion in his right lung. They are going to do some physical therapy on him to try and break that up before moving forward. It's likely that the congestion has settled there because he has been on a ventilator for so long. It's normal, but something they need to clear up before moving forward with anything else. If physical therapy doesn't do the trick, they'll call in pulmonology to see if they have any thoughts on how to get rid of it.

So that appears to be the plan today. They'll do another echocardiogram just to make sure things look good (and to see what his heart looks like in a nontraumatic situation), and they'll do another chest X-ray. But that appears to be all for the day. We'll just hope all the tests look good and that Jacob remains stable so we can start taking some steps forward tomorrow.

You know, it's pretty amazing to see all the pieces working together here. Nurses, doctors, specialists, staff, all working with parents and families in traumatic situations and doing it with grace and ease. They really have thought of everything to help make our stay here as comfortable as it can be. We can honestly say that there hasn't been a person here whom we have not been impressed with. That especially goes for our nurse. She's been with Jacob for the last five days (she's had quite a schedule). At twelve hours a shift, she has gotten to know him quite well, and was the one who called for intervention yesterday when Jacob went into cardiac arrest. She knew him well enough to call sooner than later, and probably helped to avoid anything else serious happening. So we're thankful Jacob has been with her. (Plus, she's a Red Sox fan, so we've been able to lament together this morning.)

So, we'll hope for a quiet day and regroup in the morning. Another day of rest isn't going to hurt the little man after all he went through yesterday. His cousin Molly has taken to calling him "J-Dawg" since he's been born, and so we're hoping he'll continue to show some dog-like fight and resistance (just no more stubbornness). Thanks again for your constant prayers and support. I'm sorry if this feels like reading a soap opera every day, but that's kind of what it feels like living through it (and writing about it is cathartic), so we appreciate your reading these ramblings. We'll check in again tomorrow. Until next time...

Our gift to Jacob's nurse once we left the hospital was a gift card to Dunkin' Donuts. Trivial, I know, but what do you get for the nurse who gave your son his life? Again, another occasion for which there is no appropriate section in the greeting card aisle. Every day she came in with a big cup of coffee, and so we thought we'd treat her to a few. Where words seem inadequate, those gifts seem even more so. But we had to do something. And if they made her feel anything like we felt when those gifts in the hospital were given to us, then we'd be thrilled. After weeks of sitting around and doing nothing, we leapt at the chance to do something.

A couple of years later we were in Children's Hospital taking Jacob to the Down Syndrome Clinic (an amazing program that brings patients with Down syndrome in touch with doctors, therapists, dentists, and others who specialize in treating people with Down syndrome, in one *long* morning or afternoon), and we ran into "Jacob's nurse" on the way back from the cafeteria. I confess that I didn't recognize her, but Kristen did. So I ran up and said, "Hi, do you remember us?" After looking quizzically at us for a moment (interesting to see because I imagine this is the face that I offer to people in the supermarket who know me from a wedding or funeral, but I simply can't place), she finally said, "Oh yes, of course I do." "Well, we just wanted to say hi and show Jacob to you." "My, look at how big he's gotten," she said. We engaged a few more pleasantries, said how nice it was to see each other, and went on our way.

I don't think she remembered us. In fact, I'm convinced she didn't. Amazing. The woman who is responsible for changing the course of my family's life, and to us we're simply another face in the crowd. That's not a knock on her—in fact, it's a compliment of the highest order. If the family of a child whose life she saved doesn't immediately ring a bell, it tells me that she's done the same for others as well.

That's God's hands and feet at work in this world. That's a sign that points to God. That's miraculous.

OCTOBER 21, 2008

Getting into the Rhythm

Since yesterday was pretty quiet around here, we left early and got to spend some much-needed time in the afternoon with Noah. Those few hours put Kristen and me in a good mood and helped get us into a positive mindset for what has started out (and hopefully will continue) as a good day.

Little J-Dawg (my, that caught on, didn't it?) did well overnight. Overnight Jacob's vitals remained good, and the best news is that his heart came back into rhythm! That is a really big step. He's now off the external pacemaker, and his heartbeat has come down to a more normal beat. Now the focus is on clearing up his right lung. Some tweaking of this and that, a change or two on the breathing machine, and some PT has helped, as his X-ray looked better this morning. So they've kept doing what they've been doing, and they're going to check again this afternoon. If things have cleared, we're in good shape. Otherwise they're going to do a scope (which happens right here in his room). That will give them a picture of the lung and allow them to clear out anything that may be obstructing his breathing. From there Jacob will begin taking his Viagra to reduce the pressure in his lungs (yes, it's still funny) in preparation for them to remove the paralytic tomorrow. That's the plan as we know it.

So it may not sound like much, but I think we're "getting into the rhythm" here—literally and figuratively. They keep saying that each child needs to "turn the corner," and we're guardedly optimistic that Jacob might have turned his. We're not saying that too loud and we're knocking on wood every time we say it, but we're hoping this might be an important turn. The fact that his heart came into rhythm is a big step in that direction.

(As a complete aside, but perhaps connected, before we left last night, we took Jacob's stuffed animals out of the bag we brought

them in. We haven't been able to put them in his crib with him because there's too much other stuff. However, his nurse has been using his Wally the Green Monster stuffed animal as a prop for some of the tubing. So we think that since Wally is now out of a job—with the Red Sox no longer playing—he might be sharing some of his talents with Jacob. Who knows, it might just be…)

Anyway, despite the fact that we heard that there may be snow showers tomorrow (huh? have we really been in here that long?), we're doing well today. Both Kristen and I feel optimistic about the rest of the day and where we're headed from here. Even though it has taken him a little longer than some, we're glad to see that the steps we're taking are now forward, and we hope for no more setbacks. Our nurse practitioner said that they pushed Jacob's heart hard at this end, so hopefully he'll be in better shape in a few years. So we're hoping that some bumpy days here will mean smoother sailing in the months and years to come.

I think that's all for now. I know I say it every time, but your messages and prayers mean a great deal to us. We love reading them and they really do boost our spirits. So keep those positive prayers going, and we'll hope that the next check-in is as positive. Until next time…

Levity. We needed some, and perhaps this story is ready for some as well. Kristen's niece Molly is responsible for one of those moments. Although Jacob has been given many nicknames in his short life (J-Bird, JJ, Chucky (for his love of "chucking" his toys at home), J-Diggety, but not Jake—call him that and we *will* correct you), the one that has stuck is J-Dawg. For his tenacity and never-give-up attitude, his cousin Molly aptly named him. It's a term of endearment. It's the namesake for our Buddy Walk team: the J-Dawg Walkers. It was the reason why we dressed him up as a dog in ICU for his first Halloween (yes, we were still there then). It's a name that continues to fit and continues to stick, to this day. And it provided no small amount of enjoyable posts as people found every way imaginable to work J-Dawg into a pun with their supportive posts that day. "Tell little J-Dawg to keep up the fight." "We're praying for J-Dawg!" "Blessings to J-Dawg and all the Dawg-gone family."

Wally the Green Monster as the "tube prop" for Jacob. Santa Claus and Mrs. Claus singing Christmas carols a few days later in the hallway on Halloween.

Levity. Thanks. We needed that.

I understood this need for levity from the time I spent working as a Chaplain in Clinical Pastoral Education during my seminary studies. CPE, or spiritual boot camp, as it is affectionately called, is a period of intense training for ministers during which time they work in a clinical setting (like a hospital), visit patients, and learn more about themselves and ministry that will aid them in their future work. During this time we came face to face, daily, with pain and hardship. During this time we understood the need for levity. That's why we called ourselves a "Murder of Chaplains" (a group of crows, after all, is referred to as a murder, so why not us?), and that's why Monty Python lines would fly freely in our office and in the cafeteria. *"I'm not dead yet!"* Visitors would often give us strange looks (especially if they could see our chaplain name badges), but fellow hospital workers and patient families understood. Even in the midst of the most trying and difficult times, levity is necessary.

So thanks to you all. We needed that.

OCTOBER 22, 2008

The paralytic is off...

...and so far so good (fingers crossed, knocking on wood)! Today's post is a late one because they did not remove the paralytic until about 3:30 p.m. This morning Jacob's pressures shifted a bit (not as abruptly as the other day, which was good, but enough to have people talking and Dad sweating), so they played with the settings on his ventilator, adjusted some medications, and decided to wait to take off the paralytic until just a short time ago. And, as I said, so far so good. Jacob's lung pressure (which got him into trouble last time) has looked good, his blood pressure has stayed up, and his heart rate has remained under control. Now it's a delicate balance of removing the sedation slowly (so he doesn't get too riled up) and monitoring any changes that are taking place. While doing this, they will begin to give him some food through a feeding tube and then begin to think about removing the ventilator as his body begins to breathe on its own (which should also help his breathing and pressures). All the while Wally is hanging out by his side, and his turtle and Patch Adams bears are closely monitoring (both sporting new Elmo stickers, given by our nurse, for being brave and for good luck!)

The chest X-ray from this morning showed that his right lung looked better than yesterday, but not perfect. They ended up having to do a scope yesterday afternoon, and discovered that there wasn't much blockage, but that he has an anatomical abnormality in his right lung. This is not uncommon for kids with Down syndrome and should pose no real problems for Jacob (other than the fact that he is more susceptible to things like pneumonia). Basically his upper right lung has a greater chance of collapsing, as it has done, a bit, here. However, they feel that as Jacob gets older, the lung will expand and, again, should pose no real problems for him.

Now we wait and watch what's happening. Jacob has already opened up his eyes and grabbed on to our fingers, and as I type I hear Kristen talking with the nurse about how he's starting to pull at some tubes. (Here's where the real fun begins!) They'll monitor everything very closely, and if something starts to happen, he'll go right back on the paralytic to minimize any problems. We don't want to see that happen, but it's a good fall back if he gets into trouble. However, everyone seems confident that Jacob will hang in there this time, and, of course, we're hoping for nothing less from the J-Dawg.

So, once again, thanks for your love, prayers, and support. I'll try to check in earlier tomorrow (so those of you at work can get a peek before going home), and I hope that report will talk about a quiet night, and a few more steps forward. Until next time...

As I'm reading back over this post, perhaps this should have been my first clue that Jacob was going to be every bit as feisty as Noah wasn't. Noah was, and continues to be, for the most part, a pretty mellow and mild-mannered kid. Jacob? Not so much. In talking with other families of children with Down syndrome, I have come to understand that throwing things is a common problem. Jacob, I can safely tell you, can chuck (remember Chucky?) with the best of them. Left alone, Jacob can turn a clean house (or as clean as a house can be with two children living in it) into a scene the likes of a post-tornado–ravaged Toys R Us in under two minutes flat. Seriously. We've timed him. And I have video. He's energetic, feisty, and quite a daredevil.

His "chucking," as we have come to label it, is just one of many challenges that come from raising a child with Down syndrome. Though we are convinced that he understands *way* more than he leads us to believe, Jacob's communication challenges mean that he doesn't follow directions particularly well. We can look him straight in the eye, tell him not to do something, and without blinking he'll do that very thing while staring straight at us and over enunciating the word "nooooo." It's so stinkin' cute (and hysterically funny), so as he looks at us through those almond-shaped eyes, it's hard to get mad. Of course, he doesn't get a free pass because of his challenges, but trailing him around, picking up *everything* he throws, and correcting him *every time* is exhausting. He doesn't understand the concept of an "indoor voice," which gets very interesting in restaurants. We can't reason with him and tell him that the power is out when he wants to watch his favorite show. And despite us telling him time and time again that it's dirty, sometimes lying on the rug at the bowling alley is more enticing than tossing that ball down the lane.

With the paralytic half-removed and him already pulling at tubes, I should have known what was in store for us. But Jacob wasn't quite ready for the "normal" challenges that come with developing as a child with Down syndrome. For now we were trying to see if his feisty heart and fiery lungs would take a little less paralytic and a little more of the Jacob that they were tasked with providing blood and oxygen for.

It's a good thing that his heart can control him in a way that we have yet to figure out. So far so good with another long day "Chez Children's" under our belts.

OCTOBER 23, 2008, 11:01A.M.

A Good Night

First things first, Jacob had a great night! He maintained his pressures without the paralytic, and they are very happy with what they have seen today. There's still some tweaking of this and that, but the good news is that his body appears to be ready to start functioning without the muscle relaxant. That is a great step in the right direction. So one big sigh of relief for another hurdle cleared.

The attending doctor for the day just came in and gave us the plan for today. Jacob is still on the breathing tube (and "days" away from coming off, we're told), so they'll look to wean him off of the nitric oxide he's receiving through that tube. They don't like to make many ventilator changes in a day, so that's all they'll do with that. They will also put an NJ tube into him. This is a feeding tube that gives him feeds directly into his intestine. Since his stomach hasn't really woken up enough to process the food they tried to give him yesterday, this will enable him to start getting some "real food" into him without having to work to digest it. They're also working on getting him some antibiotics for what appears to be an infection—nothing serious, but it needs to be treated nonetheless.

From here the next big step is to get the ventilator out. This, the doctor told us, could actually help his right lung expand. However, Jacob's not quite ready for that to be removed yet. His pulmonary pressures are still a bit high, so they want to make sure he's ready to go on his own before pulling that tube prematurely. Again, she said it might be "days" before that happens (which could be 2, could be 3, could be 4, we don't know— it all depends on how the little guy does).

But the good news is that the doctor now feels we're in "recovery mode" instead of "reacting mode." Those were wonderful words to hear. However, with what happened on Sunday still fresh in everyone's minds, they are going to take things very slow with Jacob—and that's ok with us.

Ok, enough of the doctor-speak already, you all want to know what he's doing, right? Well, Jacob has been wide eyed for much of the morning. Although he has somewhat of a glassy-eyed look to him (as he's still very medicated—something they'll also be looking to wean on as time goes by), he is looking around and has made eye contact with us. He's wiggling around and grabbing on to our fingers (and occasionally his tubing) at will. I was saying to Kristen that it's kind of like having a newborn again—it's been so long since we've seen him move, that we can just sit and stare at him for hours! It is a wonderful sight to behold, and we're hoping a smile isn't too far away!

So I think that's all to report from here. Each day now we'll be looking to take some baby steps forward. I keep telling myself that I need to remember Jacob's heart has been completely reconfigured, so even though it seems like it's been a long time for us, his body has to learn a whole new way to function—and that's not going to happen overnight. So as long as we're headed in the right direction, we'll be happy.

Again, thank you for your prayers, love, and support. As soon as Jacob is a bit more photogenic, we'll get some pictures uploaded for you. Until next time…

It *was* kind of like having a newborn again, as we watched Jacob open his eyes, grab for our fingers, and even pull at his tubes. We looked like first-time parents waiting anxiously for their child to open his eyes, smile, roll over, or take a first step. It was like we had embarked on a new adventure again, for the first time. And that is one of the most special things about having a child with Down syndrome—we get to enjoy those "first time" moments and celebrate them again and again. For while a typically developing child may roll over, sit up, "cruise," and start babbling in the short span of a month or two, that's usually not the case with children with Down syndrome. Each milestone takes a little bit longer to hit. As such, each milestone is reveled in and celebrated for a long time. I remember the whole family gathered around Jacob as he worked at rolling over for the first time—cheer-led by Noah chanting, "Come on little buddy, I know you can do it." And we clapped when he did it. And we clapped the next time. And the next time. And the next. Each time celebrating the accomplishment with more and more gusto. And that's because they were accomplishments. As we tell Noah, because Jacob has Down syndrome, it's going to take him a little longer to do things. That just means we get to celebrate each step all the more.

And those first steps were a big deal. For months, it seemed, Jacob had been "cruising" around the house hanging on to furniture and anything else he could get his hands on (legs, televisions, full cups of water, you name it). He then started standing up in the middle of the room unaided. When we'd make the sign language sign for "stand up," sometimes Jacob would lift his bum off the floor just a mere three inches, slam himself back into the ground with an audible "oooh," (like we would say watching a batter strike out to end a baseball game), and follow that with a loud cheer that *everyone* in the room *had* to participate in. Three inches off the ground, or all the way to standing, we cheered and cheered and cheered.

One might think that such a prolonged journey would be frustrating. "When's he going to start walking and talking," you might think we'd be exasperatedly saying to ourselves as we compared him to others. I thought that would be the case too, but it has not. We have refrained from comparing him to typically developing children, recognizing that he's his own person. We knew Jacob would progress along his own time line, and we have been fine with that—never wanting him to be anywhere but the stage he found himself in. In fact, we have actually *enjoyed* this prolonged period of development, as it has made us realize just how big each of those steps are for typically developing and differently abled children alike. And where we may not have celebrated enough with Noah, we're making it up with Jacob—with gusto.

OCTOBER 24, 2008

Slowly but Surely…

Good afternoon, everyone. You know, I have to say that it's hard not to be in a good mood as I write this update. There is a soothing harpist playing beautiful music here in the ICU for us, I'm looking out the window on a perfectly clear, crisp fall day at the Prudential building glimmering in the Boston sunlight, and Jacob is resting quietly beside Kristen and me. (Not to mention I just heard that the Deacons at church have graciously granted me a week of "family time" so I can stay here with my family next week. Thank you all very much!) It's amazing how much difference a few days make. When I think of where we were when I wrote to you on Sunday afternoon, and then see where we are now, I can't help but feel blessed—blessed for the tremendous care we have gotten, blessed for a wonderful family who has helped out with so many logistics to make these days manageable, and blessed for the love and support we have received from all of you. Thank you, from the bottom of our hearts. We're not out of the woods yet, but we do feel more blessed than you can imagine.

As you have probably guessed by now, Jacob, once again, had a great night. His pressures have all looked good. Though he's not ready for any big steps today, his lung pressure has remained at a safe level, his heart rate has been good, oxygen saturation has been strong, and his blood pressure has stayed in a safe range. In addition to this, Jacob is beginning to breathe more and more over the breathing tube. This is a good sign, and has enabled the nurses to turn down the settings on the ventilator once again. The more they turn them down, the closer he gets to coming off the tube, and the closer we get to leaving ICU. The doctor on today suggested that at this rate we might be looking at pulling the breathing tube on Sunday. They're also trying to figure out when to remove his last chest tube. But again, they'll be very cautious with all of this so that we don't have to take any steps backward.

In addition to this, they are weaning Jacob off of the real heavy duty painkillers and on to some lighter ones. They'll monitor how he does with these, of course, but the lighter drugs means that he's another step closer to not needing them anymore. They also began to feed him formula overnight. The tube, as I said yesterday, goes right into his intestine so he doesn't have to work to digest it, but he's handling it well. Yet another good sign. Other than that, it's more tweaking and fine tuning while Jacob's body continues to learn how to function.

I should probably tell you that we have been here long enough that pretty much everyone in ICU knows Jacob now. Case in point, as they began rounds this morning, the presenting nurse practitioner began her remarks with, "Well, we all know Jacob very well now"— and it's true, everyone does. We walk past nurses and doctors who have cared for him on days prior and they all ask what the latest news is; a few nurses have sought out the scheduler to be assured of working with Jacob when they're on; many have told us that his progress has "made their day"; everyone keeps poking their heads in to see him, with many remarking about how cute he is (and how they can't wait to see him without tape on his face and tubes up his nose!); and nearly all have promised to come say "hi" to us when we have moved out of ICU so that they can interact with our smiling baby boy. Certainly we're waiting as anxiously for that day as they are! So while it may not be fun to be here in ICU, they are making our stay as pleasant as possible, and for that, we are grateful. This is a tremendous place, and the people are really what make it shine.

I guess that's about all we have to report. At this point we'll take quiet and stable, because it means that we are, slowly but surely, heading in the right direction. It goes without saying that we thank you all for the prayers, love, and support. You know the drill, same Bat time, same Bat channel tomorrow, with hopefully the same good news about J-Dawg. Until next time…

A completely reconstructed heart. I mentioned that in the prior day's post, and it's something that kept coming to mind every time the doctors, nurses, and staff came in to check on Jacob's progress. While, at times, it may have felt as though things weren't progressing as fast as we might have liked them to (so, yes, true confession, sometimes I *did* want things to move along…for instance, getting out of the ICU would have been nice….), all I needed to do was stop and remember that Jacob had his heart—the central muscle in his body—completely reconstructed. A new chamber was carved out. Valves were fixed and new valves were created, all so that Jacob would have a chance of living a better life than he was with his malformed heart. That's the gift that Boston Children's Hospital gave to Jacob. Little did they know that they were giving the same gift to me.

Now granted, I did not have a physical heart reconstruction, but in many ways I feel as though I left Children's Hospital a very different person than I entered it. When Jacob was first born, we didn't know that he would be differently abled; we merely knew that he had a major heart problem that had to be corrected. And that was our hope—get in, get Jacob's heart fixed, so that then we could live a "normal" life, focusing on the things that "normal" parents focus on.

That was the last time I thought of my life—or anyone's life, for that matter—as "normal." (Isn't that just a cycle on the washing machine anyway?) Since then I have had my eyes opened to a much bigger world (which, of course, was there all along) than I was previously privy to. I can now *only* see the world through the eyes of a child with differing abilities. And this makes the world look very different. It has helped me to see that there is no such thing as a perfect child. Look beneath the surface, and you'll see that every child, every person, has their shortcomings, their limitations, their differences. While I knew this, in theory, and I could argue this point theologically, my journey with Jacob taught me to feel this with my heart—my newly reconstructed heart.

And perhaps that's why I was so passionate about our church becoming Open and Affirming (ONA) as I was when we unanimously declared ourselves to be, in May 2011. ONA, in case the term is unfamiliar, is a distinction given to United Church of Christ churches that have declared themselves to be open to, and affirming of, *all people*, regardless of race, class, gender, age, family status, sexual orientation, and physical or mental ability, to name just a few. It is a public statement and declaration made by a church that has undergone a process of prayer, reflection, and study about the ways in which churches often perpetuate the ostracizing and discriminating practices of our society against people whom the world chooses to label as "different."

Here's a portion of the sermon I preached that day:

> *"It is our practice here in this church, a few times each year, to invite the Church School children and teachers to come back into worship, after leaving for Church School, so that we, as a congregation, can celebrate communion together. When we did*

this a couple of weeks ago, it was fun to watch the kids come in—looking around as if they were doing something a little mischievous in getting to see what we grown-ups do while they are usually in Church School.

Then as the elements were served it was a joy to watch the eager and expectant eyes follow the bread and cups as they made their way toward the pews where the children sat. And then, I couldn't help but smile as Moms, Dads, and Grandparents whispered instructions to the children: "Don't eat it yet," I could almost hear them saying, "Rev. Jeff will tell us when we can eat and drink together." Joyously, I had the best seat in the house to watch all of these interactions.

But that wasn't the only thing that happened as we gathered around the table. You might recall that our youngest son Jacob—who has Down syndrome—walked up to the front of the sanctuary while all of this was happening. What you may not have seen, though, is what preceded that—Kristen and I giving each other the eye: "Is it okay that he comes up front?" "Yes, of course it is." All of that accomplished with a few raised eyebrows and subtle head nods.

So Jacob, just finding his walking legs, did make his way down front. He sat right at the foot of the table, resting his head on the step, as we shared the bread and cup. And then, when we broke into song, I bent down, picked Jacob up, held him as we sang the last hymn together, and then allowed him to greet some of you at the door before Kristen took him back over to the Parish House following worship.

Many of you afterward said that you were touched by the scene—of Dad and son standing in front of the church, singing together. And I thank you for those words, but more than that, for allowing that to happen. It was one of the most meaningful communion services I have presided over here in the church. But it's one that—if we were in a different church—may never have had the opportunity to happen....

In just a few moments we will gather together as a faith community to vote on a proposed Open and Affirming Statement. This statement is the product of two years of inquiring conversation, tearful sharing, careful Bible study, and much more. During this time as I sought to offer a pastoral ear to all of you, the most common question I heard was: 'Why do we need to declare ourselves to be Open and Affirming, when we are already?'

While I have many answers for this question, let me share just a few. First, I believe firmly that people shouldn't have to wonder whether or not they will be welcome in this place. Just the same as we say that we are a United Church of Christ congregation, we should also declare Open and Affirming plainly for all to see. For that phrase—whether you know it or not—is a catch phrase in many marginalized communities; it's one people look for on our website before they even think about darkening our doorstep.

For too often churches throw around the word 'friendly' and expect that will welcome people. Well, let me tell you that it doesn't. There are many stories of people being hurt and excluded by 'friendly' churches. I've had people share with me horror stories of that happening—even coming to me, in private, asking if it would happen to them in this place. Saying we're Open and Affirming means that we have done the work, given this prayerful thought, and have discerned who we are. That way no one has to wonder how they will be received when they come through that door.

Second, our children. We often talk about the fact that we have a growing church school here. And we do. It's a wonderful thing. But you know what? Percentages say that some of our children are gay or lesbian, some will be diagnosed as autistic, some have other differing abilities that may marginalize them from their peers. How vital is it, then, when those children are struggling in school and in life, for them to know, for certain, that they don't need to worry about whether they'll be accepted for who they are at their church? It might just be—and I don't say this lightly—the difference between life and death for a young adult who has come to the end of their rope.

And third, this is an issue of justice. If there are people in this world who are not being afforded the same rights, privileges, and opportunities as others, then our faith calls us to do something about it. Declaring ourselves to be Open and Affirming does that. It says: While the rest of the world may want to treat you differently, when you come through that door on Sunday mornings, or come to one of our gatherings, we welcome you as you are—no matter who you are or where you are on this journey of life.

My friends, today we have an opportunity to put all this in writing—to declare openly what many feel is who we are and what we're doing already. And you know what? I have to admit that this is an opportunity that has become very personal for me over the years.

When I sat down with the Search Committee that called me in 2003, I asked them whether they thought the church would be going through the Open and Affirming process some day; they said that

*they did. Since then I have dreamed of standing here, at the end of
a process well conducted, preaching these words to you. Back then
I thought I'd be doing it for you—for those of you who have been
marginalized and excluded in life—because as a heterosexual, white
male, I have had little experience walking in those shoes.*

*But today I stand here saying that I'm preaching and voting
for my family. And I would venture to guess, if we all looked at our
lives, we could say the same. That's what has become plain to me
throughout this process—Open and Affirming touches all of our
lives; and if you don't think it has yet, look closer, or just wait,
it will.*

*Personally, Jacob has changed the life of my family in such
a way that I can no longer see the world the same. I now see the
world through the eyes of a child with differing abilities. And as the
parent of such a child, if I were church shopping, I'd want to know
that he would be welcomed into the "full life, ministry, joys, and
responsibilities"²³ of participation in that church, as our proposed
statement says. Today we can vote on a document that, for a parent
like me, would leave no doubt in my mind that that was the case.*

*For Open and Affirming means that we are open to and
affirming of: the little boy with Down syndrome who finds his legs
during communion; the young man with Tourette's syndrome who
has unexpected outbursts during worship; the gay couple who are
looking for a safe space to raise their newly adopted son; the elderly
man who ambulates differently, and takes a long time to make his
way to his seat; the transgendered young adult who isn't sure that
there's a seat at the fellowship table for him anymore; the single
Mom, who can barely afford to put food on the table, and realizes
that it's going to take a church to raise her child; the young adult
who is thinking about taking her life, because her family won't
accept her now that she's come out; and the countless others whose
stories we will learn when they cross our life's path.*

*My friends, that's what Open and Affirming means. And when
we vote today, that's what we'll be saying. It's a vote that will take
only a few minutes, but it's a statement that will take a lifetime to
live out, as we strive to ensure that that gate stays open, so that,
"all," as Jesus says "may have life, and have it abundantly."*

*Today I'll be voting so that Jacob—with his newly found legs—
can walk through that gate alongside all of you. Amen."*

A completely reconstructed heart.

OCTOBER 25, 2008

A Quiet Day

*It's the weekend here in the ICU (and outside, I imagine, though I
haven't seen too much of the world in daylight lately). This means
that things are quiet around here. Jacob had a good night and has
had a good morning. His pressures are all good, and he continues
to fare well breathing above the ventilator. They said that his chest
X-ray looked much better, meaning that his right lung has improved
a good deal. They have also upped the calories on his feedings
and he is tolerating that well (save for a little mucus-driven spit
up—sorry, being here so long desensitizes you to this stuff—which a
little Zantac should remedy). So pretty much that's where we've been
since I last checked in.*

*Where we're going also looks good. The plan is to remove
Jacob's Pulmonary Artery (PAP) line soon. This measures the
pressures in his lungs. It was removed earlier and then put back in
after his episode on Sunday. Now they are feeling confident that
he no longer needs to have those pressures monitored, as they have
looked great. Barring any bleeding, this will enable them to remove
his final chest tube. This, again, should happen this afternoon. In
talking about this I asked the nurse if I needed to step out for these
procedures and she said, "No, not unless you're prone to fainting
on us." I replied, "Well, we've been through enough here that I'm
not sure anything (except what happened on Sunday) would do me
in." Her response was simple: "I can only imagine." It's been quite
a crash course in medicine and hospitals for us, one that I wouldn't
wish on anyone. But I thank God every day that such a fine facility
is here when we need it.*

*The doctor on today said that we might be looking at removing
the breathing tube tomorrow or Monday. That has us optimistic
that our stay in the ICU might be coming to an end in the not-too-
distant future. But again, that time table is all up to Jacob.*

For now I'll just sit here and watch BC football (Jacob is becoming a fan—as he will be of all Boston sports, of course; anything less is child abuse as far as I'm concerned). I'm trying to explain to him what's happening (he's very alert today) as we wait for Mom, Auntie Traci, and Mimi (Karen to the rest of you) to come in for a visit. Kristen made a trek back to Maine for us this morning, to do some odds and ends (and had to deal with tons of traffic for the commissioning of the USS New Hampshire, I hear), and so this morning has been a little Dad and son time. Here's hoping the next game Jacob and I watch together is on the couch at home where we should be!

Thanks for your devoted attention to this page and for all your love, prayers, and support. I say thank you every time (not only because not saying thank you is one of my all-time pet peeves in life), but because your support means so much to us. To my church family, I'll miss you again tomorrow morning in worship, but I hope to have a positive post waiting for you when you get back home. Until next time…

When I was in seminary I remember one of my professors coming down hard on a classmate for preaching too much about herself in her sermon. Leave yourself and your family out of your preaching was the message he gave to us. That was one of many such messages in seminary that sounded easy. (Just like not answering the late night phone call about the color of the napkins for coffee hour on Sunday, or telling a parishioner in the hospital that I'd come visit when it wasn't my day off.) Yeah, that all sounded good. It all made sense. But like so much of ministry, the reality proved to be something quite different.

I could preach about something my kids do, or say, every Sunday: Noah asking whether or not God lives in the clouds, Jacob staring out the window, transfixed by the church's carillon, Jacob's seemingly magnetic draw to sit on the church's front steps on warm summer afternoons, Noah's penchant for wandering through the church's cemetery and reading tombstones on snow days, the hugs Jacob offers to his favorite people at church (and yes, he does have favorites—right, Jon and Valerie?). Every waking moment of my day is a sermon illustration unfolding before my eyes.

And while I try hard to remember my professor's words, the congregation knows that I'm a pastor *and* a father. Sometimes I want to—and need to—bring my humanity into the pulpit. And I do. ONA Sunday was one such instance. I couldn't be the preacher that day without being the father—the issue just hit too close to home.

Yet that's not to say that I don't fret about those times when my kids are included in my sermons. While I seldom let others read my sermons before I preach them, I let a few people read the one I preached on ONA Sunday—simply because I wanted to make sure that it wasn't too much about Jacob. Those readers concurred with my feelings: sometimes you have to bring your humanity to the pulpit, and I did that day.

I'll probably never know what the right balance is. How much humanity do I bring in? How much humanity do I leave out? Where does the preacher end and the father begin? The questions linger, but one thing seems to make sense: if I can remember that I'm a father first and then a pastor, something tells me I'll be doing all right.

OCTOBER 26, 2008

Preparing to lose the breathing tube!

So, first things first—this Sunday has been a whole lot better than last week! No frantic driving in to the hospital after receiving a call from the charge nurse, no code blues, no paging the surgeon to come in to see what was happening, no frantic Mom, Dad, or nurses— thank God. It's been a very quiet morning here in ICU. We've watched the rain clouds give way to a vibrant sun now blanketing the Boston skyline, Jacob has snoozed away most of the morning, Kristen has been working on a Winnie the Pooh cross-stitch, and I am halfway through my fourth book since Jacob has been admitted (Jodi Picoult's Second Glance*—very good so far).*

(In case you're interested, the other books have been: Jodi Picoult's Mercy *(not one of her best, though I like her as an author);* Ian McEwan's Atonement *(very good); and* The Game of Their Lives *(I forget the author,[24] but the book chronicles the 1950 U.S. World Cup soccer team's upset of England—not a bad Hoosiers-like read). Kristen has finished the* Sisterhood of the Traveling Pants *series and is now reading another one—*The Last Summer*—by Ann Brashares. You'll have to ask for her opinion on those...)*

Anyway... overnight Jacob was weaned off the ventilator for six hours. He did great during this time. The vomiting he had yesterday, they feel, was due to the puffs of air he got when they were suctioning out his breathing tube (basically it caused him to get too much air in his belly). So they have been careful not to give him any more breaths than he has needed since then. This, in conjunction with some other medicine, seems to be working. No vomiting since overnight, and all his numbers have looked good.

The plan for today is to give Jacob another six-hour stretch off the ventilator. Then, they will give him some steroids (yes, that

127

rules him out of professional sports for some time) in preparation for removing the breathing tube early tomorrow morning! Woohoo! This should enable Jacob to make some real strides forward. From there, we hear, that he'll spend at least 24 more hours in the ICU post-breathing tube just to make sure all is well. During this time, we imagine, he'll lose a couple of the lines he has in him in order for him to be ready to move to 8 East—the cardiac inpatient floor (a major step down from ICU). That could, optimistically, happen on Tuesday. And we're thinking that sounds like a plan—14 days in the ICU is plenty as far as we're concerned.

So all in all Jacob continues to progress well. He has clothes on for the first time since he went in for surgery (another great sight to behold), and we're hoping for an uneventful day. Jacob and I will watch the Patriots, as Kristen keeps cross-stitching, and we'll hope for a better result than either BC or the Revolution (what a debacle) had yesterday. As I said, we're training him to be a Boston sports fan. Thank God he has a strong enough heart, now, to sit through all the heartbreak they'll bring him.

Again, thanks for the love, prayers, and support. We missed being in worship this morning, but could certainly feel the prayers wafting from north, south, and west (I'm not sure about the east... I don't know of anyone praying from boats or Europe, but if you are, thank you!). Here's hoping tomorrow's post will include some pictures of a breathing tube-less smiling baby boy for you to enjoy! Until next time...

As you can see, I needed some companions on the journey. Books work well. After all, what else did Kristen and I have to talk about, after spending countless hours together inside the ICU. And you can only say so much about the cafeteria cuisine. The highlight of our day would be when the medical helicopter for a nearby hospital landed on the adjacent roof, which we could see from our window bed. (Sad, I know, especially since that helicopter's arrival signaled some major hardship in another person's life.) Yet that's the truth. Those propelling blades and helicopter occupants were a welcome diversion. (And if you were on one such helicopter, know that my prayers were with you.)

Now why, one may ask, did we feel like we needed to be there all day, every day? The short answer is, I don't know. I just knew I *needed* to be there. I remember, vividly, the feelings I had on Easter Sunday morning (going back to Jacob's first hospitalization). I was at Kristen's parents' house taking a leisurely morning before heading into Boston, and I was going stir crazy. I watched Noah open some Easter gifts, which was great, but I couldn't stand the idea of my other son being alone on his first Easter. I told Kristen that I had to go, not giving a reason why, and I raced into Boston hours earlier than I had planned to be there. There was something sacred and intimate that I was missing by not being present with Jacob that morning. And I guess that's the best reason I can give as to why I *needed* to be with Jacob all the time—that hospital was sacred ground, and I was walking a sacred journey with my son. If I could have taken my shoes off, I would have. I wanted to be a part of it as much as possible.

And yet even though I knew God was in that space, I needed companions on that journey. Friends and relatives were great. Kristen was a rock (even if we mostly had that nontalking, supporting thing going on), and books helped to pass the time. So if you're staring at your child in a hospital bed while reading this, allowing your eyes to glimpse the helicopter landing pad, or if you've broken your reading trance long enough to listen to the "line occluded" beeping of the machine, know that I am with you in spirit and my prayers are with you too.

OCTOBER 27, 2008

No more breathing tube!

We have a late update for you today because pulling Jacob's breathing tube was quite a process! The whole team needed to be assembled in case anything went wrong (which, thankfully, it didn't). Then it was a process of removing the tube and getting him attached to some supplemental oxygen. This part went smoothly. However, in the process, they managed to pull a line out of his neck, which bled quite a bit. He was fine, but they needed to then insert a new IV, so that he could get the medicine he needs. This did not make J-Dawg happy. We spent the next two hours trying to calm him down—but oh was it nice to hear that voice again (someone remind me of this when we're home and we can't get him to stop crying!). The trick was a little sugar water and some medicine—that finally calmed him down. All in all, things went very, very well.

From here on in Kristen and I will be alternating nights in the hospital until Jacob comes home, because feedings begin tonight. He drank the sugar water very well, so we have no doubt that he'll remember how to take his bottle in no time. We just want to make sure that one of us is the one giving it to him! We've waited a long time to be able to hold him and feed him again. Which reminds me… take a look at the pictures! Now that the breathing tube is gone, we feel comfortable putting some photos of Jacob on the web. He still has a few lines—which you can't see—but his head and face look good. Everyone keeps talking about how darn cute he is (and we happen to agree)!

I'm not sure what the plan is from here. As I said, feedings start in a few hours, and I know he'll be in ICU for at least 24 hours while they monitor him post-breathing tube. So perhaps, perhaps, we'll bid adieu to the ICU either tomorrow or Wednesday—none too soon if you ask us! But really, as long as Jacob is progressing, we're happy.

    Sounds like we missed quite a day up north yesterday. No heat, no power—a forced green worship service! Noah and his Mimi and Grampy are just happy that the power came back on, so things weren't too cold for them in Maine last night—because Noah wouldn't have wanted to miss out on his school today!

    I think that's all for now. Thanks again for all the love, prayers, and support. More tomorrow... hopefully with some news about when we're leaving the ICU! Until next time...

It's true, we hadn't been posting pictures on the CarePage since Jacob had gone through his surgery. They felt like a major invasion of his privacy and ours. But that's not to say we didn't take them. We took lots of them. In fact, the digital camera card is full of pictures that only Kristen and I, and Noah and Jacob will ever see. What I was documenting in writing with these posts, we also needed to document in living color, if for no other reason than so that Jacob would be able to know his story one day.

My good friend and colleague Beth, who is differently abled, spent a large chunk of her early years at Children's Hospital, having numerous surgeries and procedures done. Some of those she remembers. Some of those she knows about only because the scars on her body tell a story that her brain is unable to remember. And yet, she wanted to know that story. When she was growing up, she wanted to understand what each scar and mark meant, as if they were a road map that connected her past to her future. Her parents' pictures enabled that to happen for her, and she told us to make sure that would happen for Jacob. When he looks at the long scar on his shoulder from his aortic arch procedure, when he looks at the scars on his wrist from medicine lines, when he sees the remains of holes in his belly from other lines, and when his eyes follow that long scar down the center of his chest that opened him, and us, up to this world we were now living in, we needed to be able to tell him, and show him, the story.

And so we have pictures of a medically paralyzed child. We have pictures of breathing tubes, and heart monitoring equipment. We have pictures of an ICU room. We have pictures of lines running in and out of him. We have pictures of scenes that most families would never want to be privy to, let alone remember. We have pictures that will never go into a photo album that we'll leave lying around the house for visitors to peruse. We have pictures that will only be taken out in moments as intimate and holy as those we shared by his bedside in ICU, as we help Jacob learn his story, and as we seek to never forget it.

After all, his scars are our scars. For every mark he has on his body, we have corresponding marks on our souls. And since those scars are the roads that have led us to a deeper communion with God and with each other, they're pictures we'll cherish forever.

OCTOBER 28, 2008

We're movin' on up...

... to a de-luxe apartment in the sky (a free Elmo sticker—sorry, that's all we have here) to the first one who posts where that line is from!). Ok, so it's not a deluxe apartment, but it is outside of the ICU! That's right, Jacob will be heading out of the ICU tomorrow. That's the news we got today. He could probably manage fine today, but, as always, they're taking things slow with him. Which is fine, as far as we're concerned.

Last night they decided to give Jacob a break and just give him IV fluids. His throat and belly were not up to much more, they thought. However, this made for quite a cranky night. So we pushed a little this morning (and talked to one of the doctors we like) and he got them to speed up giving Jacob some food. And boy was he happy about it! He had 100 milliliters of food in his first oral feed (to put this in perspective, his good feeds at home were only 120 milliliters). So he was hungry, and he didn't forget how to eat one bit! After a good after-dinner belch, Jacob laid down for what has been—and continues to be—a long afternoon nap. We knew some food was all he needed, and we anticipate a smiling baby boy (or at least a hungry baby boy) when he wakes!

So what else is happening... Jacob was weaned off of the nitric oxide they have been giving him through his oxygen tube. He's on straight oxygen now, and that should be weaned this afternoon. And he will be losing the arterial line that he has in his foot later today. That will leave him with one IV in his head (which they need to give him meds) and two lines in his chest (which can be hooked up to the external pacemaker should he need it—which we hope he won't!). Neither of these have to be removed before he goes across the hall. So that means, when they're ready, Jacob will be ready!

Once we get out of ICU, we anticipate that things will move pretty quickly from there. We'll learn how to bathe him, pick him up (carefully because of his chest incision), dress his wounds, etc. We're also hoping that his new digs will mean that Noah can come to visit his baby brother. He would have been allowed in the ICU, but we chose not to scare Noah by exposing him to such an intense ward. As it is, he's mostly interested in riding the elevators here ("the purple ones, to floor 8, and then back to floor B," he'll tell you) and playing in the playroom across the hall. But really it will be good for him to see that his brother is all right.

So, and I can't believe I'm actually about to type this, but it seems that our journey may be coming to an end here soon. We'd love to say that we'll be home by the end of the week, but we know better than to plan ahead or get our hopes up. Playing this one day at a time is what has gotten us this far, so we'll keep that mindset for now. We just know that soon we will all shout "Dy-no-mite" (yes, that's a clue for above) when we cross the state line into Maine. Soon, we hope, very soon.

So thank you, again, for all your love, prayers, and support. We're hoping today will be a quiet one from here on out—with many chances to feed our boy, in between watching the Prudential building disappear and reappear behind the dark rain clouds swirling throughout Boston (believe it or not, there's actually blue sky here now!). We have added a couple of pictures for you to look at—so enjoy—and hopefully tomorrow's post will show Jacob in his brand new space! Until next time...

One of my colleagues told me (after the fact) that she was focusing all of her prayerful attention during our situation on Noah. "He's going to need prayers too," she said to me, "and I'm sure Jacob will be receiving plenty." It was an incredibly gracious gesture, on her part, and incredibly appreciated. During this entire hospital stay we were "camping out" at my in-laws' house about twenty-five minutes north of Boston. Seeing as staying there cut off a good forty-five minutes from our drive back to Maine, and my in-laws made great Sherpas, it made sense for us to set up our base camp there. Not only that, but it gave Noah some good, quality time with his grandparents, cousins, and aunt and uncle, while our attention was directed toward Boston. And he handled this time incredibly well.

He was going for a couple of weeks without seeing his brother, seeing his parents for limited periods of time each day, traveling from

Massachusetts to Maine to be in school (though frequent stops for munchkins did ease that burden), and yet he took it all in stride. His preschool teachers were amazed at how well he was doing. And he seemed okay with our story that Jacob's heart "boo boo" was taking just a little longer than expected to heal.

I'd have to say that those prayers worked. I'd have to say that Noah was the blessed recipient of God's love—with the channeled love of my colleague wrapped up in God's love as well. And it makes me think, again, that God had a plan in mind when Jacob was born into our lives—a plan that included the birth of such a compassionate child some two plus years before Jacob's extra chromosomes appeared. How that all works, again, I have no idea. I just give thanks to God that it does, and that we are the blessed beneficiaries of two amazing children who have made us, and will make each other, better people.

It seems unfair that we should be so richly blessed.

And yeah, yeah, yeah. Before you say it, I know. I'll admit that my CarePage clue reveals that I mixed up *Good Times* and *The Jeffersons*. I'm blaming it on too much sterile ICU air. That's my story, and I'm sticking to it.

OCTOBER 29, 2008

Not so fast…

It's day 15 here for us in the ICU, and, unfortunately, it looks like we're going to be adding more to that tally. Despite the news we shared yesterday, it seems that The Jefferson's song might have been a bit premature. Overnight Jacob spiked a fever and was having some trouble breathing—his respiration rate was high and he appeared to be straining (or "pulling" as they call it) when he breathed. This, despite the fact that he had a couple of great feeds from the bottle yesterday. What this means is that Jacob has now been put on a more high-powered oxygen (in hopes of helping that right lung a bit, as that's still part of the issue). They have stopped us from giving him food orally—since they feel that's too taxing on his system—and instead are using the feeding tube again. Today they'll add some steroids to the mix to hopefully help the breathing situation. All of this means that we'll be hitting day 16—and possibly more than that—on our ICU tally board.

Needless to say, this emotional rollercoaster has been trying on all of us. Case in point: Late last night I received word that we were going to be transferred within an hour, believe it or not, only to find out that this was not the case. Upon waking this morning, we learned that he wouldn't be moving today either. There's no way around it; it's frustrating.

So it looks like there won't be much happening here today. They've got Jacob's pain medication at a good level, so he's comfortable, but sleepy. We won't be feeding him, but he will be receiving some chest therapy in hopes of breaking up whatever is in his lungs. Apparently it's a matter of more watching and waiting as we give Jacob the time he needs to get fully healed.

In the meantime some prayers for patience would be helpful. This has been trying on all of us—Kristen, Noah, Jacob, and I—as well as on our family, whom we have relied on, heavily, to help us

136

out. Noah is itching to get back home (and not really understanding why Jacob's heart is taking so long to heal), and Kristen and I would love to get our lives back to normal. All in due time, we know, but the waiting is the hard part.

So again, thank you for your continued support. I apologize for the less-than-jovial post, but as I'm sure you can tell, today has been a tough one. Here's hoping we have some better news to share with everyone tomorrow. Again, thanks for all your love and prayers—it's what has gotten us through, and what will continue to in the days ahead. Until next time…

Everything I Learned About Life with a Child with Down Syndrome I Learned First While at Children's Hospital." That could easily have been the title of this book. Looking back on these posts has revealed just how much of Jacob's journey at the hospital is a metaphor for the life that we have lived with him. As we saw in the ICU, what seem to be steps backward are sometimes steps forward, and a few positive steps forward seem to be always followed by a step back. Jacob's schooling is an example. When Jacob turned three, the in-home Early Intervention services—the ones we had *so* desired and had been provided to him by the state of Maine—came to an end. A good thing, perhaps, as we were, admittedly, frustrated with their not-always-dependable services. There were times when Jacob would go two or three weeks without seeing one of his therapists. This always meant, after a few encouraging steps forward, a couple of steps back.

Now we heard that we (strike that "we" and insert Kristen) were going to have to make a forty-minute trip—each way—to bring Jacob to a developmental preschool some thirty miles northwest of us. We weren't sure if it would start right away. We didn't know what kind of services he'd receive there. We were convinced that this was going to be another time of regression for Jacob.

It wasn't. Not in the slightest.

They had a place for him almost right away. And after an expectedly rough first couple of transition days at school, Jacob flourished. He learned to walk. He started to sign and babble more. He began to feed himself (a bit). He showed an interest (which is now an obsession as I write) in listening to story books read to him. He learned, and enjoyed, baby yoga. He started to do crafts with his classmates. He made friends with the other students and teachers. He developed in amazing ways that we just didn't see coming—at least not so rapidly.

Then we heard the news that with the new administration taking over in Maine, budget cuts were on the docket—and Jacob's school was a prime target. It makes sense, right? Why spend *all that money* on schooling for children to help them become contributing members of society? Why not let them flounder at home and then become a burden to the state and their families *later* when things will just cost more money? Makes sense, doesn't it? And this, so that a budget can be balanced and the wealthiest residents of our state can receive bigger and bigger tax cuts. Logical, right? Don't get me wrong, I'm not looking for more than anyone else—I'm just looking for all to be treated equally, and for our country to live out Jesus' call to "care for the least of these" in our midst. Until we start seeing health care and social services as a right and not a privilege, that's never going to happen.

All we knew was that Jacob's school was up for budget cuts, and we didn't have a clue how that would affect our family. Fifty percent of the services could be gone, we were told. Fifty percent of the services that had helped our child develop faster in a couple of months than he had developed in years at home! Fifty percent! In the end the cuts amounted to about 10 percent, but there are still more politicians hopeful that number can be raised. Steps forward and steps back.

There's also Jacob's feeding. A few months ago it wouldn't have been an uncommon sight to see Jacob sitting on the couch next to Kristen, chomping on a piece of pizza with her. We assumed that this meant that he was well on his way to eating the foods that a typically developing child would. Add to this the fact that he started drinking milk on his own out of a cup with a straw, and we were convinced that we were headed in the right direction. The right direction? Not so much.

Today when we put pizza in front of Jacob's face, he normally whacks it away. If we manage to get him to take a bite, he normally spits it right back out, or tries to swallow it whole without chewing. If we put other food on the table in front of him, he throws it. And while he is drinking milk on his own, he normally gulps it down in one sip before throwing his cup behind the television or over the couch or with expert aim at Noah's Lego table. This before letting out a very impressive belch or two. And yet he will sit and suck ketchup off a French fry or frosting off a spoon like there's no problem at all…hmmm….

Steps forward and steps back—all in a day in the world of raising a differently abled child, and all in a day in the world of raising a typically developing child. In some ways those worlds aren't that different at all.

"Everything I Learned About Life with a Child with Down Syndrome I Learned First While at Children's Hospital." Translation: Just when we thought we knew what to expect, we didn't. We weren't headed out of the ICU—not for some time yet.

OCTOBER 30, 2008

Day 16…Same as Day 15…

So as you can tell by the title, there's not much to report today. They are now in the mode of watching Jacob to see if his breathing gets better. His respiratory rate seems to be pretty good, but they want to continue to keep an eye on him. He's on a three-day course of steroids (which will end tomorrow). That, plus the high-powered oxygen and the chest therapy, they hope, will clear up the problem. Until then, we wait.

So rather than drone on about being frustrated as I did yesterday (sorry about that, it was just not the news we expected to hear), I'll talk about our ICU digs, which, by now, have become pretty comfortable to us (if you're not interested in reading, feel free to skip to the end!).

In the back of the room there's a window mattress (euphemistically called a bed) which looks out—if you get real close to the glass—at part of the Boston skyline. In the morning the sunlight streams in our window beautifully. Directly across from us is an office building, below we can see part of the Children's Hospital garden, and above to our right is the helicopter landing pad for Brigham and Women's Hospital. Although we don't like to see the helicopters arrive (because it means someone is in trouble), it is always interesting to see the pilots maneuver the crafts onto that tiny landing spot. And I have to say that it's nothing like you see on ER. Once the copter lands, people don't race out with their heads ducked. They all seem to wait until the blades have stopped before they exit—a good plan if you ask me, though not very exciting for television.

The room is much bigger now that the ventilator and most of Jacob's medicines are gone. We told you that he was on 11 medicines when he came in. These were all in little machines behind his bed which would beep on and off all day long (syringe near empty, line occluded, dosage done, etc.). Now the only thing hanging behind him is his formula. He's still getting fed through the feeding tube, but now it's going into his stomach— instead of his intestine—which will keep his stomach working. His medicines (save for one painkiller which he gets periodically) all go in manually through his IV or feeding tube now. There's a big monitor above Jacob's bed which, right now, shows his heart rate, oxygen rate, and oxygen saturation level. His blood pressure is now taken manually every 30 minutes, and that number appears on the lower part of the screen. The nurses have a computer right in the room to update all of Jacob's activities, medications, etc. (I'm dying to know if there's solitaire on there, but I haven't checked.) Plus they have a little window that peeks in on us from a computer terminal in the hall. It's kind of like we're in a fish tank and being watched all day long (but hey, we live in a parsonage and know what that's like!).

Our ICU room is down the end of a hall, room number 8. Past us is one room and then the corridor is closed off for renovations. They're adding another 2 rooms to the Cardiac ICU, because this place is always full. In fact, patients are being treated in other areas of the hospital because there's no room for them here. When Jacob finally vacates, his room won't stay empty for more than a few hours before another patient, and another worried family, occupy our spots, as they begin a journey not unlike (but hopefully not as long as) ours.

Down the hall we have a pseudo-kitchen at our disposal. There's apple juice and cranberry juice, ice cream, and popsicles. There's also supposed to be graham crackers and saltines—but we have someone here who hoards the graham crackers, I think, as that bin is almost always empty. By now we have met a good number of the doctors and nurses here, so we get smiles and "hellos" as we walk down the hall. Nurses we've had in the past keep coming in to look at Jacob to see how he's doing and remark at how good he looks. Even the folks who work at the ICU desk have come to know us—as they just buzz us in without asking who we're here to see, and give us a hard time when we go to the cafeteria but don't bring them back a coffee. Again, everyone here works hard to make things as comfortable for us as possible.

So it is here that we will watch and wait another day. (Hey, if things are boring tomorrow, maybe I'll give you an update on the cafeteria—now won't that be fun!) Jacob is in the best medical

hands in the world, and we know this will all end… someday.
We're staying patient (those prayers are working, thank you), and
just counting our blessings that Jacob will come out of this in the
end, much better than he was before. When we first heard of Jacob's
diagnosis, we just hoped and prayed that his problem would be one
they could fix. It was, and they have—now we just need to wait for
the dust to settle.

Kristen will be making a trip home tomorrow to take Noah to
school for his costume parade. He's going to be a fireman. Jacob
was supposed to be a Dalmatian to go along with him. He won't be,
but we might just try and slip his costume on here in the hospital
and get some pictures of him for you. As an aside, his cousin Lexi
wanted to be a part of this, so she decided that she was going to be
the supermodel that Noah and Jacob had to rescue from a burning
building… because supermodels are always caught in house fires,
you know… those of you who know Lexi won't be surprised. Noah
will miss trick-or-treating in Maine tonight, but Kristen will take
him out with Lexi tomorrow night at her parents' house. Here's
hoping he sends some good candy my way!

So thanks for reading. Not much to say about Jacob, but I
figured I ought to give you something, since you took the time to log
on. Again, thanks for the prayers. As I said, the ones for patience
seem to be working, so please keep them up. We'll check in again
tomorrow with hopefully something new to share. Until next time…

Catharsis. Diversion. Something to pass the time. Call it what you
will, but these posts (now getting somewhat gratuitously long, I
know) became as much for me as they were for Jacob and our family
and friends, as those days turned into weeks in the ICU. I found them
to be healing and helpful. I was shocked and surprised that people
actually wanted to read them—and not only that, but they found them
meaningful (even the hospital "tours" strangely enough). In so reading,
the seed for this book (little did I know it then) was planted.

I'll share just a few of the responses to the post above:

"Thanks, Jeff, for taking the time to keep us all posted. I hope these
postings are printable for you to take home as a journal about this
remarkable journey. You write so well, and these memories are precious.
Here's hoping that this part of the trip is coming to a happy end."

"Hi Jeff and Kristen, I'm still with you guys, thinking of you and baby
Gallagher all the time. I'm taking Luna to her card [appointment] tomorrow
morning myself. Jeff, your writing is amazing, and reading your posts puts

me right back in the ICU, I know how hard (and intensely boring) it is. But as you said, there is comfort in knowing the team really knows what they are doing. Sending hugs your way."

"Hi Jeff and Kristen. The daily updates are great. It keeps us all posted and, yes, it does allow you to vent. The coaster ride is hard—many ups and downs. I pray that the ups are for longer periods of time and the downs will become less. Jeff, are you able to get out for a run? You need to care for yourself as well as the family. God Bless."

"Good to hear from you, Jeff. Your detailed description of your setting reminded me of how very intimately I got to know the 4th floor of Mercy when my husband…was there for 10 very long days. When I went back recently to visit my brother-in-law, the very tiles on the hall floor said to me, "Well, hello…we've missed you." When you're in that situation with a loved one, everyone and everything is your intimate friend…It brought back, too, the mixture of tension, fear, gratitude and a sense of abiding grace that was a part of me nearly losing my loved one."

"Hey Jeff—have you given any thought to writing a book about all this? You definitely have The Gift and I think it would be a helpful account of Jacob's journey…Happy Halloween to you all."

Scary thought, even for Halloween—writing a book about all this? Reliving those days in the ICU? Walking down those sacred halls in my memory again?

Never say never.

Speaking of these posts and responses, a while after we returned to Maine, our congregation threw a combined birthday party for Noah and Jacob. I crassly referred to it as the "We-Can-Finally-Celebrate-Because-Jacob's-Not-Going-To-Die-Party." This was partly in jest, though partly very serious. Although the congregation's heart was in the right place—and we are *incredibly* grateful for their generosity and their efforts in making that party happen for us—it does reveal, again, that we, as a society, don't really know the social protocol when it comes to babies who struggle to get their lives going. I'm just grateful that, regardless of when it happened, the congregation realized that Jacob's birth needed to be celebrated—and they made it happen.

At that party one of the members of the congregation gave us, perhaps, the sweetest gift we received—a printed copy of every single CarePage update and response to date. It was special—not only for the amount of ink and paper that she used on us—but because she recognized that this was a story that we needed to savor.

And another seed for this book was planted.

OCTOBER 31, 2008, 1:48 p.m.

Happy Halloween!

So I guess there are worse places to be on Halloween. Those of you who know me well know that I think this is one of the most absurd holidays out there (Sorry, Halloween lovers—but dressing up to wander around and get candy from your neighbors? Come on, what's next, a bunny giving out eggs in the spring?); however, I do have to say that it's been kind of amusing here in the hospital. Many of the staff members are dressed up (as everything from brides, to cowgirls, to Superman). Jacob received a beanie baby dressed up as a ghost yesterday and a Halloween balloon today along with a Halloween heart. Outside the ICU, apparently, kids get to dress up in costume and go around the hospital trick-or-treating (the Cardiac ICU desk is a stop, but the kids cannot venture inside). There's also a costume parade, I hear, but I haven't seen anything happening. It's kind of isolated over here in the ICU, so I may just have to venture out from time to time to see if I can get a glimpse of what's happening. We'll have to see.

Jacob had another quiet night. As you know, little changes have been the order for the last couple of days. They are weaning him down off the high-powered oxygen (hopefully by the end of today—assuming his numbers look good). They have moved him from IV pain killers to oral. This doesn't sound like a big shift, but it is—many kids have a hard time with the transition (as Jacob did earlier, you might recall), so the fact that he seems to be handling it well this time is good. Once he goes back to regular oxygen we should get to feed him orally again—tonight, or tomorrow, likely. It's all a matter of watching his breathing now. They think that he might have had an inflammation of his bronchi in his lungs, and possibly some inflammation in his throat from the breathing tube being in so long. Steroids, and time, should do the trick, there's really nothing else they can do. The Docs think he looks good today (less pulling when he breathes), and a couple of people have whispered that we might be out of ICU by the end of the weekend. But you'll hear no more Jeffersons songs from me, I've learned my lesson.

So, now for what you really want to hear about: the cafeteria. (Same rules apply, skip to the end if you don't want to hear about Children's cuisine.) If you ride the elevator down to floor "B" as Noah will tell you (the same floor you come in on), you're on your way to the cafeteria—although you might not know it, it's kind of a maze of halls to get there. And, really, it appears as though you're going somewhere you're not supposed to when heading down (especially since there is no ceiling to cover the wiring in one of the hallways. You'd think, in the best children's hospital in the world that they could install a drop ceiling, but I guess not. I guess they're just spending their money on the patients and technology—not a bad thing).

Once you enter the cafeteria it's hard not to notice that there are no windows (which means on sunny days, it's not a popular destination). It's in the basement, so location makes a view of the outside world kind of tough. Along the walls are pictures of turtles and other sea life along with some facts, like: the floor of the cafeteria is made, partially, of seaweed, we are eating 200% more broccoli than we were 6 years ago, and the largest tomato every grown on a vine was over 8 pounds (that's a lot of pasta sauce if you ask me, or a lot of ammunition for one really bad joke... I'd better watch out). During lunchtime the place is mobbed—with doctors, nurses, and staff occupying many of the spots. At dinner it's a ghost town—with just a few visitors looking to find a tasty tidbit to tide them over.

(Ok, random aside inserted here... while typing I was just serenaded by Santa Claus and Mrs. Claus singing "happy holidays to you." They stopped to say hi and ask me why there's so much orange and black and so little red and green around here today. You know, if I didn't know any better, I'd guess that some of that morphine Jacob was getting has found its way into my water.)

Anyway, back to the cafeteria (as I assume my best Phantom Gourmet voice)... there are ample selections to choose from, which change from week to week, a nice touch. There's a pasta and pizza station (disappointing, because I love pizza, and it's pretty lousy). Then there's a station to make wraps and sandwiches—a good option, when nothing else hits the spot. There's the chef's corner,

*which rotates everything from an Oktoberfest spread (full of kielbasa
and German coleslaw), to a Pu-Pu platter bonanza, to seafood stir
fry (today's cholesterol-raising option). This station is hit or miss.
Nearby the soup is a good option (though nothing like Sara's), but
only if they're serving clam chowder. After that there's a salad bar—
which is ok, but pales in comparison to Warren's.*

*Then there's the entree of the day (which is always way more
food than you'd want to eat at lunch), and a grill station—hot dogs,
hamburgers, chicken fingers, curly fries (a good option), and some
special meal of the day (it was a citrus salmon burger the other day,
not great, but edible). In between there's a Green Mountain coffee
station, a place to buy yogurt and fruit, and a limited selection of
drinks (you'd think they'd have decently flavored water here, but
it's hard to come by). All in all, it's not a bad take, though you'd be
surprised how quickly all those choices become bland.*

*Just up the street from Children's is a food court which we have
just recently discovered—with Subway, a burrito place, Chinese
food, and the like. Nothing to write home about, but it's something
different. If you're headed there, be sure to swing by the Harvard
Coop across the street. They have a great selection of books, and
pretty much anything you want with a Harvard logo on it (though
they all seem to say Harvard Medical, I wonder why...).*

*That's about all I can say. Not as exciting as yesterday, I
realize, but it is a cafeteria after all. Even John Updike would
struggle to make this place sound interesting (though he'd
undoubtedly make it sound more risqué). I'm sorry to say that
there is no mystery meat here, but there are plenty of hairnets to go
around.*

*We have some photos of Jacob in his Halloween costume, but
they won't be uploaded until tomorrow. Kristen took the camera
home with her to photograph Noah's Halloween parade and
excursion tonight with Lexi (who isn't going to be a supermodel after
all) tonight. So we'll get those uploaded tomorrow. Once again, we
thank you for your love, support, and prayers. I'll have to think of
something to entertain you with tomorrow, but rest assured that I
will refrain from describing the bathrooms. Until next time...*

Halloween has always baffled me. Why do we want to dress up
in scary costumes to scare one another? Isn't the world a scary
enough place as it is? If we're only talking about Dalmatians and waiting-
to-be-saved-supermodels and firemen walking around grabbing candy

145

from their neighbors, then I'm okay with it. But ghosts and ghouls and goblins and gremlins? Thanks, but no thanks. I don't need to be scared any more than life has already scared me.

And, to be fair, Jacob has done little to allay those fears. I fear the challenges and trials that may come his way. Children with differing abilities are more prone to being picked on and excluded in school; Jacob will likely have a harder time getting through the education system than typically developing children do; I fear the funding he needs for special education programs may not be there when he needs it; I fear further health challenges, as people with Down syndrome are more prone to diseases like leukemia and other complex and scary medical conditions; then there's that whole heart thing, to go along with all of the traditional fears that parents have for their children.

So there's *plenty* to keep me scared. I just choose not to let fear rule my life. I choose not to be afraid of bringing Jacob bowling (where he'll take too long and might look awkward), or out to dinner (where he'll make too much noise), or to church (where he—gasp—might actually walk up to the communion table!). I choose not to let my fears about Jacob's differing abilities limit his experiences in life. I could keep him sheltered all day long—from the I'm-not-sure-how-they'll-react world outside—but I don't.

I don't let fear rule my life in the same way that I don't let fear rule my theology. "Repent! Believe in Jesus! Confess him as Lord and Savior to avoid God's punishing flames of hell" (insert bloody Jesus cartoon here). No thanks, I'm good. You'll never hear me preaching a theology that scares people into believing, or into living the way that God has called us to live. The gospel writers tried that (just read John), and I don't think it's a particularly effective strategy for encouraging faithful living.

I choose to share stories that show how God loves and accepts all people—not in spite of their differences, but *because* of their differences—even the little boy with Down syndrome who tries to run down the lane after the bowling ball. For I believe that when people learn of, and experience, God's love, they'll be moved to respond in ways that a fear-based theology just can't inspire.

But what about all that the Bible says about fear, some may ask. For example, Proverbs 9:10 and Psalm 111:10 both say: "The fear of the Lord is the beginning of wisdom." So aren't we supposed to fear God? Well, it's all in the translation. Instead of a knee-knocking, Halloween-like fear, in many instances the word fear should be better translated as "awe," "wonder," or "reverence." The latter is the preferred translation of the above texts, with the added dimension that such a reverence is intended to "[motivate] righteousness."[25] In other words, we are motivated to do good not because of fear of what will happen if we do not, but because such is the way we live in response to something that fills us with enough reverence and wonder to take our breath away.

So I don't let fear rule my life, my family, or my theology. As for Halloween? No thanks. I'm good. There's enough in life to scare me already, and I choose to focus my eyes in a different direction.

NOVEMBER 1, 2008

Halloween...the day after

Yes, I realize that the title sounds like a poorly written and acted horror movie (but then aren't they all... cue the ditzy blonde who thinks that it's a great idea, when a storm knocks out the power and she's home alone, to race into a dark corner of a basement to investigate a "strange" noise... sorry, I'm not a big fan of horror flicks either, or haunted houses... remember, I went to college and taught in Salem, where Halloween doesn't have very many fans at all... yes, yes, I know, I'm waiting for the Halloween lovers' bashing to begin again...), so please just be happy with the fact that I brought Halloween into the title again for all of you to sentimentalize about yesterday. You can thank me later. Enough already—grab your candy everyone and read on! (As an aside, Jacob's cardiologist was in yesterday and he told us that he and his wife allow their kids to eat all the candy they want on Halloween; then, when they get sick, they no longer have to worry about how to get them to stop eating it—problem solved!)

As many of you know, in religious circles today is All Saints Day, a day to pause and remember those saints of old who have gone before us. I can't help but think of the many family members Jacob has watching over him here, as well as all those unknown saints who helped make this hospital into the wonderful place that it is. We certainly are indebted to them for being able to be here and receive the incredible care that we have.

Last night was a good one for J-Dawg. He was very cranky yesterday afternoon, so his night nurse and the charge nurse conferred and decided that he might be hungry. Apparently, even though he was being fed, continuously, on the feeding tube, he was only getting about one ounce an hour. That meant that while he was getting enough nutrition, he might have been feeling hungry.

So around 9:30 p.m., Jacob got a bottle and wolfed down four ounces in no time flat. He then proceeded to sleep—happy as a clam (because we all know how happy clams are!)—until 5:30 a.m. I fed him again in the morning and that set the tone for what has been a good day. Jacob seems much happier today and has handled the food well. Plus, since he came off the high-powered oxygen last night, we're another step closer to leaving the ICU. They did say to us that they seldom move kids who have been here as long as Jacob on the weekend, so I think we're looking at Monday, at the earliest, for our ICU exodus. (But I'm not saying that for sure... we all know what happened last time.) We'll just be happy with some more steps forward and leave it at that.

Which leads me to this: apparently I've set up quite the expectation among our loyal readers. Many of you have commented that you're enjoying your guided tour of Children's (and yes, the tour guide will accept donations at the end!). So I don't want to disappoint any of you, but neither do I want to describe the bathrooms (sorry Judy Mitsui). So instead I'll say a little about the sounds of Children's Hospital.

Interestingly, the Cardiac ICU is one of the quietest wards at Children's (of course, I say this as Jacob is crying because he doesn't want to burp). The reason: nearly all the kids here are on breathing tubes, so crying isn't a sound you hear very often. Most move out very quickly after they have been extubated. Actually, the most common sound to hear is the rhythmic—almost symphonic at times—beeping of empty syringes, occluded lines, heart rate leads falling off, and oxygen indicators that are not picking up. Occasionally a blaring Destat alarm breaks the rhythm, only to be followed by an unhooked ventilator singing a creative little number. Kristen and I can now tell, by the sound of the beep, whether Jacob's leads have fallen off, his medicine is done, his numbers have fallen out of acceptable levels, or whether we need to get up and find the nurse. More often than not, when our nurse happens to be out of the room, and an alarm bellows, another nurse will come in to help out, and we'll tell them what's going on without having to look at the screen. In fact, the thing the nurses do here most often, I think, is to hit the pause alarms button on the computer screens, to stop the symphony from droning on too long (and yes, as I wrote this paragraph, Jacob's oxygen level wasn't registering...beep...beep... beep).

These noises are interrupted, occasionally, by an intercom voice coming from the main desk, from time to time—and there's a code to this, we've figured out. In addition to announcing phone calls and who's answering a page, people are asked to "walk" to a certain room—this means that their presence is needed, but not urgently. However, when they are told to "go" to a room, they hightail their way down the hall to wherever they are being paged. The only thing that tops that is when a "code" is called. Code Blue means there's a medical emergency of an unknown type—and this makes people run. (Again, thankful that we weren't here to hear Code Blue Cardiac ICU Room 8, from a couple weeks ago.)

Once out on the floor the beeping is a little less frequent (less medicines being given), but the overhead pages don't cease. My favorites are: "Environmental services to room..." (as I always I wonder if someone is moving, or if someone is about to have to clean up something they really don't want to), and also "If anyone is looking for a volunteer, please have them call..." (I always envision a volunteer causing trouble at the nurses' station, prompting them to want the volunteer out of their hair!).

Ahh, yes, the noises of Children's... CD release date coming soon (but the occluded line ringtone is already available, I hear!)

Anyway... that's all from here today. If you hear beeps in your head all day long, don't blame me, you chose to keep reading. Which reminds me, I should answer a few questions that were posed in recent messages by some of you... First, there is a Harvard Coop across the street. We are in Boston, so this isn't "the big Coop" in Cambridge. It's sort of a satellite Coop. Yes I have been able to get out running while I've been in here. Most of my runs have been at 8 o'clock at night, after Noah is in bed, which is interesting as the streets of my home town have changed, quite a bit, since I last sauntered down them. And finally, there are no plans for a book, yet, but if I choose to write one, I'm expecting you all to buy :)

Halloween photos have been uploaded, check them out! And as always, thanks for the love, prayers, and support. I immensely enjoy writing these reflections, and I'm glad there are a few of you who enjoy reading them. Until next time...

If writing was saving grace number one for me during this time, then running was a close second—a very close second. I was a "runner" in high school. I use that term loosely because I really just ran track to stay in shape for soccer—my true love. After putting on more weight than

I'd like to admit during college and graduate school, I took up biking (to drop the first pounds) and then running after I got to a comfortable weight, shortly after Noah was born. And what I found was amazing. Running cleared my head. It allowed me to unpack, or prepare for, the day. It gave me an adrenaline rush that my body came to crave (a friend calls it his "healthy addiction"). And when Jacob was in the hospital, it gave me the chance to beat up my body in a way that enabled my frustrations to be pounded out, one step at a time.

I'd go for runs late at night after spending all day in the ICU. I'd have my headlamp and reflective vest on, and just run—wherever the Spirit and my legs led me. I'd run away the sadness. I'd run away the pain. I'd run away the frustration. And I'd run to connect with God and achieve the sanity that I so desperately searched to find in those hospital rooms in between writing CarePage entries. Running gave all this to me, and more. And so I vowed that I would use running to give back.

It just so happened that I saw a message come across one of the Children's televisions one afternoon. It advertised the "Miles for Miracles" program—a fundraising program whereby runners procure elusive spots in prestigious races and, in the process, raise the critical funding Children's Hospital needs to do its work. I vowed then that I was going to do something that I had dreamed of doing, when I was in high school, but never thought I'd actually achieve: I was going to run the Boston Marathon.

And so, just about one year after Jacob's second hospitalization, I was accepted as a member of the Children's Hospital Miles for Miracles team. I put pen to paper. I agreed to raise the money, and I knew there was no turning back—I'd be making the 26.2 mile trek from Hopkinton to Boston that I'd seen thousands of runners complete on television. And I'd be doing it for Jacob and our good friend and fellow patient at Children's, Justin. I'd be doing it for Children's. I'd be doing it to say thank you for all that they, and running, had given to me.

I trained through the harsh New England winter months. I ran long runs of fifteen, sixteen, twenty miles plus in negative wind chills on snow and ice-covered streets. And every mile—as painful as they became—felt like a miracle. I never forgot whom I was running for, or why I vowed to undertake this challenge in the first place.

After months of training—and a not-quite-as-sleepless-night-as-the-night-before-Jacob's-surgery—Marathon Monday arrived. I donned the multi-colored Children's Hospital singlet proudly. I toed the line (actually, you don't ever "toe the line"—in fact, you start about a quarter to a half-mile down the street from "the line"!) and I set off. In retrospect I either didn't drink enough water or trained too hard leading up to the race, I'm not sure, but my time wasn't what I wanted to be. Hitting mile 18—just before the infamous Heartbreak Hill (which is actually the final in a series of increasingly large hills), I cramped up. My legs would hardly move. It was almost funny (if it didn't hurt so much)—my mind was saying, "Keep going, this is the Boston Marathon," and my legs were saying, "Hah! Not on your life!" I knew that my goal time—of four hours—was not going to happen. But really, in the end that mattered very little. Running a marathon, for me, was about pushing my body and mind beyond what I ever thought would be possible—and doing it for such a great cause made it all the better.

As I struggled to cover those last few miles, I knew that my family would be waiting for me at mile 25—and that kept me going. As I passed by Boston College (and people kept passing by me) and made the left-hand turn onto Beacon Street, the emotions got me. Had I not been wearing sunglasses, racers and spectators alike would have seen that my eyes were full to overflowing. Had they not known better, they would have assumed they were tears of pain. And they were—but not for the reasons they'd think.

They were tears of pain, yes, but also tears of joy, tears of frustration, tears of elation, tears of thanksgiving, tears of every emotion that I had felt on that journey with Jacob—and they all came flooding out some two miles before the finish line. I became so choked up that my already-labored breathing became worse.

When I approached my family, I ran near to hand off my fuel belt. I didn't say anything, and I didn't stop—because I knew the emotions would overwhelm me, and I would never finish the race. Instead I let their cheers propel me on, as the tears finally fell onto my cheeks. So much emotion, and I was letting it all go, step by painful step.

When I finally crossed the finish line—sacred and holy ground for me that day, even before it became equally as hallowed for the world after the bombings in 2013—my emotions were in check. I raised my right fist, slightly—about as much as I could—and gave thanks that the race was over. With my finisher's medal on, blanket wrapped around my shoulders, and water bottle in hand, I made my way with a friend and teammate, who also ran for Jacob and Children's Hospital, to the Children's postrace meeting area. I was in too much pain then, but as the days wore on, I was finally able to truly give thanks that I raised over $10,000 for the hospital that saved my son's life.

Where words of thanks failed, I can only hope 26.2 miles made up for it.

NOVEMBER 2, 2008

Sabbath Rest

Well it's Sunday again, and like the good pastor I am, I haven't been to church for three weeks now. (I think I have a good excuse, though.) I'm just glad that our church's worship services have been in the very capable hands of Jack and Diane (sounds like a John Mellencamp song... "a little ditty about Jack and Diane..."). Today our church celebrated its 294th birthday—on Heritage Sunday—only 6 more years to go until the big 300! (And to think, the building doesn't look a day over 250!)

Anyway, Jacob had a great night. The feeding tube came out—making his mother very happy (as she's been saying, "He's not going home with that thing, you know")—and Jacob has been eating like a horse, seriously. He's actually eating more now than he was before the surgery! I'm sure that's because he's feeling better and his body is working more efficiently. Remember, pre-surgery Jacob was having a hard time getting the oxygen he needed to do anything—especially eat. Now he's got plenty, and he's shown that through his vociferous way of telling us he's hungry. Man can that boy belt out a cry!

In between feeds Jacob has been snoozing away, and being the playful, smiley little man that he was a few weeks ago. I said to Kristen just yesterday, "It's nice to see the kid we brought into the hospital again." It's been a long road for J-Dawg, but I think he's finally back, pretty close, to where we want him. As I said yesterday, if this wasn't the weekend, we may well have moved across the hall today. But it is Sunday, and so we'll just take it as a day of Sabbath rest.

Now, we have some family coming in soon, so I need to keep today's post short, but I've had a few requests for the next stop on our virtual tour. So today I will spellbind you with a tour of the parking garage... ohh, ahh! After turning off Storrow Drive, and driving by every baseball fan's Mecca—Fenway Park—Children's Hospital is just around the corner. (It's in the medical district, near Beth Israel Deaconess, Dana Farber, and Brigham and Women's.) Just across the street from the main entrance to Children's is the lovely parking garage. It's eight levels high. If you could drive it fast enough up or down, it might feel like an amusement park ride—because you get so dizzy—but alas, traveling in it is never that quick.

If you can arrive prior to 6:30 a.m., then you're usually in good shape to grab a spot on the 2nd or 3rd level. If not, you're looking at 6, 7, or even the penthouse suite—the 8th level rooftop. Parking is insanely expensive. 24 hours will cost you $35.00. Want valet parking? (Not that we ever have.) Then you're looking at over $40.00. Mercifully, if you're a patient or parent at Children's, then you get to park at the discount price of $9.00 per 24 hours. Not bad, but that adds up after a while. The spaces in the lot are so tight together that an inch or two over the yellow line—either way—means that you might not be opening your car door. A couple of times we've contemplated climbing in through the back of Kristen's car to get into the driver's seat! Turning the corners inside is no picnic either, and forget it if there's someone coming the other way.

But that's where we get to park. Upon leaving at the end of the day you're greeted with a woman saying, "Please insert your ticket, stripe up…" and she always thanks you twice as you exit (she ought to offer a foot rub, for the amount it costs, as far as I'm concerned!). After that it's a left out of the exit (so you don't crash into Bertucci's) and into the joyful world of downtown Boston traffic! Yeehaw! (Have I mentioned how nice it is to live in Maine lately?)

So there's your parking garage tour—riveting, I know! Just so you know, from here on out updates are going to be a little less regular. I start back to work tomorrow, so I'm not sure when my schedule will allow me to write. It might be in the evenings, mornings, I just don't know. I will do my best, though, to keep these updates going for as long as Jacob is here—and for a little beyond.

Of course, we thank you, again, for all your love, prayers and support. If I don't remember to say it, get on out there and vote on Tuesday—especially in Maine, because we are the only state that does not award our electoral votes winner take all. And New Hampshirites, you too—you're a swing state. Jacob has told us that he's voting the same as his Mom and Dad this year. I won't say who that's for—because I don't want to get into a political debate here—but anyone who's seen the sticker on my car, or knows my political *and social stances (cough, cough... liberal) will know which box I'm checking. Until next time...*

I haven't said a lot about Kristen thus far, and that hasn't been an oversight—I just don't know where to begin. As a pastor's wife, Kristen understands (ad nauseum) what it means to be put in awkward situations, suffer through things you don't necessarily want to suffer through (read: your husband complaining about work, talking theology with friends, book manuscript editing, etc.), and manage to show grace and ease through it all. (Yes, that is an apt job description for a minister's partner.) Thank God she's my best friend. Jacob's trials were no different. Having worked in a pediatrician's office for over ten years, Kristen, mercifully, would be able to navigate us through the maze of insurance company issues and loads of paperwork that would follow Jacob's hospitalization, as she had in the past. It should have been a sign to me that she was going to be Jacob's greatest advocate and ally in life.

Take, for instance, Children's Sunday at our church when Jacob was three years old. As a toddler Jacob had shown a real disdain for large groups of people laughing and clapping. Such incidents would set him off on a crying spree that was always hard to bring him back from. Other loud noises didn't seem to get to him (strangely, like cowbells at our premarathon reception), yet laughing and clapping always did him in.

So it was on Children's Sunday that Kristen anticipated a lot of both—clapping for the students and laughing during what was usually a pretty lighthearted and festive affair. The laughing, of course, couldn't be controlled—but the clapping most certainly could. The day before the service Kristen told me that she was making an executive decision for Children's Sunday—there would only be applause in sign language allowed (arms raised in the air with hands twisting back and forth). She did this for Jacob, of course, but also, I think, to help the congregation understand what it was going to mean to live up to that ONA statement.

After all, ONA wasn't simply a declaration we made so that we could have a fancy certificate on the wall, it was a declaration that we made that said that we were committed to making the worship life of the church as welcoming a place as it could be for all those who choose to worship with us. For those who have difficulty hearing, we have sermons printed out that they can follow along with; for those who have trouble ambulating, we have a ramp leading up to the front door; for those who have trouble sitting in our nineteenth century pews (not for those who enjoy napping), we're working on pillows. For Jacob we decided that we could do without clapping.

And so our service went off without a hitch (or should I say without a clap?). Everyone welcomed the change (with some even coming up to me after worship to say that they preferred it), and the congregation got a little taste of what it means to live out our ONA policy. I've said before that I don't think God *causes* certain children to be born to specific parents. Yet these are some of the *many* reasons why I think that Jacob got not only the mother he needed, but the mother he deserved.

Yes, God. Still listening.

•

NOVEMBER 3, 2008

New Digs!

*So a new week brought with it some new digs for J-Dawg…finally!
After 19 days in the ICU, Jacob decided it was time to head across
the hall to 8 East! Woohoo! It just so happens that the big move
was while I was at work this morning (perhaps I should have gone
back to work sooner, huh?). Regardless, it was nice to come in this
evening, not have to get buzzed in to see my boy (or to get buzzed
in and out to go to the bathroom), and see Jacob asleep in his new
space.*

*I have to say that it's a great room. We have the window seat
(which is wonderful) and it looks out over the main entrance of
Children's (Kristen saw me walking up the sidewalk as I came in
this evening). It's a straight shot to Logan Airport, apparently, as
Kristen has been watching planes come and go since Jacob moved
at noon time. Just the fact that we have a new address now is a
good thing. And if Noah gets to come in to visit, he'll be a happy
camper—Jacob's door has a Thomas the Tank Engine poster on it
(Noah's favorite).*

*So the plan from here on out, as I understand it, is to watch
Jacob. As long as he eats well and doesn't spike a fever (which he
has already done, thank you very much), we'll get out of here soon.
As far as the fever goes, Jacob is having his urine tested just to see
what's up. Kristen thinks he's fine. It's warm in his room, and Jacob
is like his Dad—he likes to be cool all the time. So it may just be that
he overheated a bit. We shall see. So they'll watch him and decide
when we finally get to get out of here. Some are saying mid-week,
some are saying the end of the week—we're just hoping it's before
Thanksgiving!*

*Now, the part you've been waiting for… Kristen came up with
the tour stop for today… the television! Now, I have to say that*

we have watched very little television here. Kristen has been cross-stitching and doing puzzles until the cows come home, and I have been reading and doing a fair share of puzzles myself. However, the TV is interesting. For the most part, you get the channels you'd want—the major networks, sports channels, etc. But there are also a few special "treats" if you click around enough.

There's the relaxation channel, which often shows pictures of waterfalls and waves lapping up on the beach with soothing music in the background. (Apparently there's also a scary guy who tries to walk you through meditation exercises. I haven't seen him, so you'll have to ask Kristen what that's all about!) There's my favorite channel—a still camera on top of the hospital. It doesn't move, doesn't pan, doesn't shut off, and there's no music. It's just a straight shot off the roof of the hospital—24/7. My guess is that it's so you can see the weather without having to look out the window, but really I have no idea, and I can't imagine actually watching it.

Then there are the music channels. I've heard more Hall (our new neighbor up north) and Oates, Jefferson Starship, Huey Lewis, Billy Joel, and REO Speedwagon this week than I have in a long time! It's not bad to have in the background, though. As the music plays, various screens pass by. We have had it on to stimulate Jacob a bit since it's pretty colorful (not that we advocate that much TV watching, but staring at the ceiling is pretty boring after a while!).

So let me give you a taste of what you can see on the channel. In addition to kids' drawings of the Hulk on top of the hospital, information on parking (see yesterday's post), the movie list for the week (four/day for young kids and four/day for teens and young adults—so far we've seen The Lion King, Cars, Angels in the Outfield…), information about blood donation, where to eat, and where to worship, there are the fun facts of the day! Get a pen, you might want to write these down!

You blink over 10,000,000 times each year (tax dollars hard at work paying someone to figure that one out). Ducks' quacks have no echoes—nobody knows why. Eskimos use refrigerators to keep their food from freezing. Disney World opened on October 1, 1971. The Children's Hospital OR is open 24/7 and does over 20,000 procedures each year (yeow—makes you realize that a donation to this hospital is a good thing, which you can do at www.childrenshospital.org, if anyone's interested… which we will be doing, as we've done in the past, once we pay all our bills!).

So that's about it from here. It was nice to be back to work, see a few of you, and get out for a run on familiar streets. I'll be here tonight so Kristen can go home and see Noah, and she'll be back in again in the morning. I'll make my way back up 95 to work, vote, and spend the evening watching the election returns in Maine.

In the meantime we'll keep hoping for good news from Jacob. We'll let you know about the fever (we're sure it's nothing), and whatever else may be happening. I know you're all itching for a tour of the chapel, but I confess, I've only been there once (just to peek in) and that was early, early on. I'll try to get back to give you the lowdown sometime soon! Thanks for all the love, prayers, and support. I'll post tomorrow when time allows—I'm just not sure when that will be! Until next time...

I finally went back to work. I knew it had to happen sometime, and although the congregation had been incredibly gracious in giving me the time off that I needed to be with my family, that time had to come to an end. It turned out that showing up for work was the easy part; the hard part was, what would I do when I got there? Now, truth be told, many pastoral duties are set in stone each week: answer e-mails (loads of e-mails), attend meetings, prepare and write the worship service, sermon and bulletin, etc., answer more e-mails. So that part I was okay with. But the rest of the pastoral duties are incredibly amorphous: sit at the bedside of a parishioner dying of cancer, offer pastoral care to someone whose marriage is deteriorating, visit people in the hospital (egads, that place again?), be an ear to bend for anyone who needed it, perform a funeral for a cat you never met (that's a story for a different book), fix the toilet in the church, among thousands of other things. How was I going to do that when my body was at work, but my heart and mind were in Boston? And wouldn't everyone just want to talk about Jacob anyway? How was I going to be effective in doing my job?

Well, let's start with the last question first. It was true that everyone did want to talk about Jacob. And so, when I was with someone, for the first few minutes we would talk about Jacob, and then I, not too subtly, would suggest that the conversation needed to turn to them. It's amazing how someone going through personal struggles can shift their attention to someone else, isn't it? A good diversion if nothing else. And therein lies the answer to that first question: How did I pastor while Jacob was in the hospital? It's simple, I just didn't think about it.

Now that sounds pretty crass, but in CPE (remember Spiritual Boot Camp?) we were taught to be able to compartmentalize our lives. In other words, when we walk into a patient's room and see them hooked up to oxygen, heart rate monitors, and breathing tubes, it's not going to be helpful if my mind suddenly shifts to thinking of Jacob. As my CPE instructor put it: You need to get your shit out of the way to be able to minister to the person who needs to be ministered to. (At least that's how I interpreted what he said, though I'm pretty sure the expletive is right!)

So I learned to place my problems in a separate part of my heart and mind. When walking into a hospital room, when presiding over the funeral for a beloved parishioner who reminded me of my grandmother, when talking with a family about their joyful and healthy baby boy who was about to be baptized, while doing a Christian funeral for a Buddhist cat (yes, definitely a different book), I simply got out of the way. I assumed my role as a companion on their journey. I practiced active listening. I tried not to put my foot in my mouth. And I tried to be the best pastor I could be.

It turns out that it worked. I was able to be present in trying times, even as my life was one big trying time. I was able to find the words to pray beside the sick and celebrate the joy of new life as I would have been able to if my life was going along swimmingly (but then, who can really say that anyway?). It turns out that it was a good diversion. I was able to get lost in caring for another, and let go of my own challenges for a while. I was (at least I think I was) the pastor that the church needed me to be.

Yet that all changed when I closed the door of my office, walked across the driveway (long commute, I know, but you should see the squirrel traffic), and entered my home. Once I opened that door, Jacob was once again at the forefront of my thoughts. I became the prone-to-tears, heart-wrenched father that I was in Boston. A layperson might say that I was faking it until I made it through. And I'd have to say that they were pretty much right on.

NOVEMBER 4, 2008

Going for a walk?

That's right, believe it or not, J-Dawg may now be able to go for walks! That's the latest news we received today. He had the external pacing wires removed (they were the ones that hooked Jacob up to the pacemaker early on in ICU). Following this, he has to be hooked up to the monitor for an hour. But after that Kristen is free to unhook the little man and take Jacob for a walk. This is big news. He'll be much happier with a change of scenery, as lying in that bed for three weeks straight, no doubt, has gotten quite old. And we'll be happy to be able to get out and stretch our legs too! Apparently we'll have free reign to take Jacob where we want (just not out the front door, yet, for obvious reasons!).

As you can probably tell, then, last night was a good one for Jacob. He slept all the way through (that's our boy!) and although he was a little fussy when he woke up, he settled down nicely. He had a great bottle for Kristen late morning just after having a chest x-ray. They did a urine analysis and didn't find anything related to the fever he had yesterday—which is great. So for now they'll just chalk that fever up as one of those great "unknowns" and hope it doesn't happen again.

Tomorrow Jacob is scheduled for an echocardiogram. They're hoping to be able to do it without having to sedate him (so we'll hope he's quiet and doesn't move around much). If they can't get the pictures they're looking for without sedating him, then they'll have to prep him for a sedated echo on Thursday or Friday. This will likely increase his stay in the hospital, so we're hoping he'll cooperate tomorrow. And what they see on the echo should go a long way toward telling us how much longer Jacob will be in Boston.

That's really about all the news we have. I'm back working today (after spending the night with the J-Dawg), so this is all as related by Kristen. It was nice to spend a night outside ICU, though,

I do have to say! Jacob has a little girl as his roommate. She's 13 months old and from Ohio. She's had two heart surgeries (like Jacob) already, and is in for a catheterization because her veins keep collapsing and will not allow sufficient blood to go to her lungs. Amazing, isn't it? As I said, there are hundreds of stories floating around that hospital everyday—ours being just one of them.

So it was good to have a roommate, good to have no beeping (all the beeps happen at the nurses' station, not in individual rooms), and good to sleep on something that more closely resembled a bed than that lousy excuse for a mattress in ICU! So just as Jacob moved up in the world, I guess our accommodations did as well.

No guided tours today, sorry, I've got lots to do at work, and you should be out voting, not staring at your computer screen! The polls were busy in Kittery, which likely means a good turnout all over.

Thanks again for your love, prayers, and support. The tour will resume tomorrow, I promise, and we'll hope to have some good news about a successful—and good looking—echocardiogram. Until next time…

Sophia. That was her name. The little girl in the bed beside us in Children's. At Jacob's age they don't mind mixing the sexes. And for Kristen that turned out to be a good thing. She and Sophia's mom hit it off quite well—with each mother intimately understanding what the other was going through. As I said, there are stories to be told all over Children's Hospital—just as there are in hospitals and homes all across the world. So what makes Jacob's story so special then? Nothing. And everything. And that's exactly the reason why I felt so compelled to write this book.

As a pastor, each and every week I pick up the same book, read the same stories, and prepare to preach to, mostly, the same people. Yet in a miraculous way, those familiar, biblical stories—even the ones that have been preached on hundreds of times before—are specific, yet general enough, for nearly every person in the pews to be able to identify with. For in hearing those stories—shared some two thousand years ago— something always seems to hit home. A stay-at-home mom identifies with a Galilean fisherman. A former high school football standout has an affinity for the short-in-stature Zacchaeus. A still-grieving father connects with a weeping Mary and Martha when Lazarus has died. Some stories, clearly, are easier to identify with than others. And yet, more often than not, the people in the pews find a way to connect.

Preacher and author Harry Emerson Fosdick notably said: "No one comes to church to find out what happened to the Jebusites."

And it's true. No one comes to hear biblical exegesis. What they do come to church for is to hear a story that will intersect their own, to hear emotions that mirror theirs, to hear a challenge to inspire them through their week ahead. And good preaching makes that happen. When the words are spoken, and infused with God's Spirit on their way to arriving in a listener's ear, something special happens—something *divine* happens. It's something that makes a two thousand-year-old story about uneducated fishermen on a boat become incredibly pertinent to a high-powered CEO.

I hope and pray and *believe* that is true for Jacob's story as well. You may not know anyone with Down syndrome, you may not be a churchgoer, you may never have set foot in Maine, you may not have any children, and yet this story has intrigued you enough that you're still reading so close to the end. In this way, Jacob's story is Sophia's story. Sophia's story is Luna's story. Luna's story is Noah's story. Noah's story is your story, and all the stories are God's stories—God's stories for God's children, who have the power and the potential to teach and inspire us all.

Just think, all that and you still didn't find out who the Jebusites are.

NOVEMBER 5, 2008

Another change of scenery coming?

Ok, so on the day after the United States voted for change, Jacob may well be following suit. The news we got today is that they are starting the discharge paperwork for Jacob! That's right, let me say it again, they are starting the discharge paperwork! Ok, I'll say it slowly—dis-charge pa-per-work! Discharge paperwork! Woohoo! We don't know if it will be tomorrow or Friday—it all depends on how things progress tonight and tomorrow—but it is coming, and we are, to say the least, excited about it.

Basically what they want to watch is how Jacob's oxygen saturation levels look. He's on either no oxygen or an extremely low level of oxygen right now. When he's awake his numbers are great, however, when he sleeps, the numbers drop a tad. He never falls into a dangerous level, but it's below what they'd like to optimally see— so they just give him a boost from time to time. (For example, he's asleep now, on just a touch of oxygen, and his saturation is between 88–92%; without it, he falls into the low 80s while sleeping—not that different than where he was before surgery, but not where they want him.)

A little before lunch today Jacob had his echocardiogram. They were able to do it without sedation, which was wonderful. Jacob cooperated very well (apparently he's itching to get out of here too!), with just a helpful little distraction from the nebulizer. The pictures they got came out good and the repair looks great. They said that pressure levels are evening out and although the heart is not working perfectly yet, it's well on its way to where we want it to be.

Maybe tomorrow, maybe Friday, that's all we wanted to hear.

At this point it's possible that Jacob could come home on some oxygen (though I don't think that's too likely). He will definitely be coming home on a couple of pain killers (which we will wean him off over time), Lasix (which reduces the fluid around his heart), Zantac (to keep his food down), Albuterol (given through the nebulizer to lessen his congestion, and everybody's favorite, Viagra (to reduce the pressure in his lungs). (And yes, we have thought about how interesting it's going to be to describe this to him when he's older!) It's quite a list, but Kristen has become an expert at giving meds by now, so it doesn't bother us a bit.

We just want Jacob to come home. Maybe tomorrow, maybe Friday—that's all we wanted to hear.

In my last post I said that I would pick up with my hospital tour tonight. I confess, as we're heading closer and closer to discharge (and as I have less time sitting idly by a hospital bed), I'm less inclined to keep the tour going. However, I did try tonight. After grabbing a quick bite to eat for supper, Kristen and I walked over to the chapel—you know, the one that we hadn't set foot in since the day of Jacob's surgery. I poked my head in, prepared to take a few notes, but there was a Muslim man inside saying his evening prayers.

Not wanting to interrupt his spiritual discipline, I decided that the tour could wait. It seemed kind of silly to interrupt him just so that I could poke around a bit. So it may just be that you'll have to imagine the chapel yourselves—as, with any luck, I might not have time to get back there before we head on up Route 1 and Route 95 and cross the Piscataqua River bridge back to our home in Maine.

So I guess that's it for tonight. Not much more to say, which is a very, very, very good thing. With any luck, we'll be home and these CarePage updates will become few and far between. But rest assured, even when everyone is healthy, we will update from time to time, with pictures of the boys and updates as to what's happening. But we'll hopefully be done with these daily bedside updates very soon. Now, let me take a moment to shift off track just a bit. Regardless of your political affiliation, I think we can all be proud of the fact that this country has elected the first African-American president, just some 40 years after the civil rights movement ended. That's history to be proud of; hopefully, Jacob will make his own tomorrow. Until next time… (P.S.—there might be something unique about today's post… hint, hint… big kudos, and maybe another Elmo sticker, to anyone who figures it out!)

It turns out Jacob did end up coming home on oxygen. In much the same way as we were tutored in how to run the feeding machine that was our "take home gift" from hospital stay number one, this time we got a crash course in oxygen tanks. No smoking (no problem there), no candles (uh-oh), here's how you set the gauge, call before you run out, make sure you put the "oxygen in use" sign on your front door. We listened to the instructions, but it didn't matter, we figured. Jacob would probably use oxygen for a week or two, maybe we'd need one delivery to get us through, and we'd be on our way.

Once again, not so fast. One to two weeks turned into six months during the daytime hours, and ten months at night while Jacob slept. Monitoring oxygen levels became as much a part of our daily routine as changing diapers. The boy who once had a feeding tube taped to his left cheek would now get raw on both sides from the new nasal cannula tape. And once again we had pictures—that no family wants in their coffee table album—to document our latest dark-forest phase in our journey through the wilderness.

But we almost didn't make it home. On the day we were leaving Kristen had tickets to take Noah to a Disney-live show with her sister and Noah's cousin Lexi. When she bought them we both assumed that Jacob's surgery and hospital stay would be a distant memory by the time the show rolled around. Instead it was the night we were headed home. "I'll be fine," I said, prepared to take Jacob home by myself for a little Dad and son bonding time. Good plan, I thought. The problem was that the three-foot-tall tank (there were no travel-size tanks to be had) didn't quite fit into the back seat of my car like I had envisioned. Wondering if I was going to need to drop down the back seat of my sedan and run the oxygen cord through from the trunk or perhaps strap it to the roof of my car like some futuristic race car, I finally managed to push the passenger seat all the way back and prop the tank up between the seat and the dashboard. With the oxygen cord snaked through the head rest to connect with Jacob, and my hand steadying the tank all the way home, the three of us—Jacob, me, and our unexpected metallic-green copilot—finally made our way north to the land of twenty-foot-long oxygen cords wrapped around the house, and a front porch menagerie of oxygen tanks.

Weeks later I became privy to a sight that I never thought I would see. With a travel-sized oxygen tank in my left hand, and Jacob's car seat in my right, we made our way to my brother's house for a family gathering. Upon setting Jacob down in the living room, and taking a few steps back to remove my coat, the sight before my eyes was stunning: my grandmother, seated in one chair, oxygen tank to her left, and Jacob, lying in his car seat, oxygen tank to his right. The Alpha and the

Omega plain as day in front of me. The beginning and the end of life joined together in oxygen dependency and medical vulnerability. Safe to say that it was a bond that I never thought my son and grandmother would share.

When my brothers, Tom and Greg, and their wives, Diana and Jen, along with Kristen and I, made our way into the hospital ICU room a year later to say goodbye to "Nana" for the final time, that image was in the forefront of my thoughts. With Nana unable to speak because of a breathing tube down her throat, and surrounded by all those familiar beeps and bells and smells, those helpless, bedside feelings from Children's Hospital came rushing back to me. I didn't see it then, but in looking back now, the message was as clear as day. Yes, Jacob's life was precious and vulnerable, but so too was my grandmother's, so too was the man in the ICU bed in the room next door, so too were all of ours standing at her side, saying our goodbyes. Life—precious and vulnerable—a gift for however long we have to live it, and in whatever unique way we were created to experience it.

The National Down Syndrome Congress has a catch phrase they use—"More alike than different"—to describe the relationship between those with Down syndrome and the rest of the world. I couldn't have picked two more different people to help me see that the wilderness had just showered me with another blessing.

As for "the riddle" from the CarePage posts? Take the first letter of each paragraph and it spells out: "Obama wins." Guess I just revealed my political leanings—as if you hadn't guessed yet!

NOVEMBER 6, 2008

Looks like one more day...

Since I haven't been in Boston since early this morning, today's update is going to be a brief one. Although we haven't gotten the "official" word yet, it appears that Jacob is going to spend one more night in the hospital. We've been talking all along about how his lungs (not his heart) have been holding him up, and it appears that that is the case again today. Jacob's oxygen saturation levels are a bit on the low side. Again, it's not to the dangerous level, and it doesn't happen when he's awake—just when his body settles down as he's sleeping. His oxygen levels drop, and although he manages to rally well pretty quickly, it's not where they'd optimally like to see him.

So it appears that Jacob will be coming home tomorrow with oxygen. We're not sure if he's going to need to wear it all the time, of just when he's sleeping (we imagine they'll tell us tomorrow). And we know that this isn't a permanent thing. Once out of Boston, Jacob will continue to be followed by his cardiologist up north, and his pediatrician in Massachusetts, and both will be able to tell us how his oxygen levels look. As they look better, we imagine, we'll get to bid adieu to the supplemental oxygen once and for all.

So that's it, really. I'm back at work plugging away on worship for Sunday, and Kristen will be spending the night in Boston with J-Dawg. Being outside the ICU is nice, because we now have a roommate to talk with. I think I mentioned before that the patient in the room with Jacob is a 13-month-old girl from Ohio. She recently came up to have a cardiac catheterization. In doing that they discovered that the blood going to her lungs is extremely poor. So she's going to have to undergo what amounts to, essentially, chemotherapy (even though she doesn't have cancer) to try and solve the problem. The good news is that the effects on her will not be as bad as an adult on chemo; the bad news is that there's no guarantee this will work, and even if it does, it's only buying her some extra time before she'll need a lung transplant. As I said, there are hundreds of stories in Children's every single day. We're just one of them—and are blessed that Jacob's problems are limited to what they are, and correctable.

So while a general prayer for children in the hospital everywhere can't ever hurt, I encourage you, whenever you go into a hospital, drive by a hospital, or are celebrating a holiday at home with your healthy family, to just remember that there are hundreds of people—in Children's alone—who could use your prayers, 24 hours a day, 7 days a week, 365 days a year. Again, it's no fun being there, but thank God the facility is there when people need it. You can rest assured that for the rest of our lives, Children's will receive our support—for the wonderful work they've done for Jacob, and that they continue to do for all those children whose stories we've yet to learn.

Here's hoping we can get you a photo of Jacob back home or en route to Maine tomorrow (and perhaps one of the two boys together). No-one was able to figure out the "uniqueness" about yesterday's post. So here's another clue to help you out: "Add up the beginnings for a reason to celebrate." That's all you're getting. Good luck.

Thanks, as always, for your love, prayers, and support. Until next time…

On the back of our bulletins every Sunday morning it lists the staff of the church. It has my name as pastor, our organist's name, our administrative assistant's name, and the contact information for each of us. And below all of that it says: "The entire congregation, ministers." Now rest assured that I do not have an entire congregation full of ordained clergy (God help us all!). We have a congregation that is made up of everyday people that you'd meet anywhere across the world: carpenters and creative artists, musicians and manufacturers, retirees and retail workers, with, yes, a few ministers thrown in between. And everyone's job is, very much, to be a *minister*, in that it is *everyone's* job to be a minister of the work and word of Jesus Christ. Children's Hospital—whether they do so consciously or not—are exemplars of this.

From the moment we walked into Children's for that very first ultrasound, long before we knew the extent of what we were dealing with, we were treated like royalty. Whether the staff or the doctors were having a bad day at home, they never let it impact their work. They treated us with care and respect, and they tried to make some of the most difficult-to-swallow days of our lives just a little more palatable. As Jesus might say, they offered a couple of cold water to the parched and thirsty souls before them, and in doing it to us, they did it to Jesus. That's ministry.

Walt Disney World was the same way. When Jacob was about a year-and-a-half, our family took a vacation to the happiest place on earth—a place that certainly entertains its fair share of people with unhappy stories. From those there on Make a Wish-funded trips, to those who are battling inner and outer turmoils and illnesses, not everyone there is as "happy" as they may appear to be. But they are enabled to be happy because of how well they are treated, or, as I would say, *ministered* to. As one Disney cast member puts it, in Christopher Perry's book, *The Church Mouse:* "These kids have to struggle every day of their lives to do things other people take for granted. I will do everything I can to make sure their time here is as magical as possible."[26] If that isn't a statement of ministry, then I don't know what is.

Now we are lucky. Jacob's differing ability is visible for people to see. Although we often fail to notice his characteristic Down syndrome eyes, nose, and facial features, that's not the case for many we come into contact with. Many times we have been stopped in the grocery store (or just the other day, at Children's, by another mom whose daughter has Down syndrome), to talk about Jacob. They make a special point of coming over and talking to us and admiring him—that is, those who can look past the baby with the feeding tube. We learned quickly that Down syndrome made us all members of an exclusive club.

Disney cast members are members of this club by proxy. Every character we saw and every staff member we came into contact with made a special effort to come over and see Jacob. In fact, we have a picture of Jacob having breakfast with the characters with a somewhat-irritated father in the background who felt that they were lavishing too much attention on Jacob. We didn't feel guilty at all. We enjoyed being ministered to.

Whether practicing Christians, Buddhists, Muslims, or atheists, the folks at Disney and Children's know how to embody a love that can only be described, in my book, as *divine.* They are the ministers that I hope and pray that our congregation and I can be. They did it for everyone (even the somewhat-irritated Dad's family). They did it for Jacob. They did it for the least of these. They did it for me. And they did it for God. That's about as good as ministry gets.

NOVEMBER 7, 2008

Shipping Outta Boston!

With all due respect to the Dropkick Murphys, we're not Shipping Up to Boston, we're Shipping Outta Boston! I've had that song in my head all morning (along with the Grateful Dead's "Truckin'", you know the song with the line "What a long strange trip it's been"... gee, I wonder why!). Anyway, enough of the musical banter, the good news is that Jacob is all set to come home! Today! Woohoo! And New England has rolled out a dreary, gray fall day to celebrate... yes! That's ok, things will be bright in the Gallagher house tonight.

So the plan is for Jacob to get a chest X-ray this morning (just so they get one more picture before he leaves), and then to ship on out. All the paperwork is done. Apparently part of the reason why he stayed last night was so that they could work out the logistics on getting him oxygen and getting him approved for the Viagra he'll be taking. As we said before, he'll be coming home on a whole host of meds; but that's ok, it's nothing we're not used to by now. Kristen is in Boston with Jacob this morning taking down all the discharge instructions. If you've ever been in the hospital, you'll know that it's quite a stack of paper they give you—with medications listed, follow-up appointments scheduled, etc. So I'm glad it's her taking down all the info and not me :)

Now we'll get a chance to get Jacob home and settled and get him cranking on the Early Intervention programs for his Down syndrome. EI had already come in and assessed Jacob, but wanted to wait until after his surgery before moving in to decide what therapies he might need to help him develop. So they'll look at his speech (as much as they can at this point), fine motor skills, gross motor skills, etc., and determine what help he might need in the days and months ahead. Everyone tells us that kids with Down syndrome do very well when EI gets started early, so we're excited to get things going with Jacob to see how he progresses.

Since we're coming to the end of these daily posts, I have a couple of tidbits that have been floating in my head for a few days that I'd like to share with you. The first is especially geared to my church family. You know how I'm often preaching about the importance of sharing our faith (you know, evangelism, that dreaded "e" word that has been corrupted by the religious right, but really just means sharing good news, not ramming your faith down someone else's throat)? Well, the other night I was talking with Jacob's nurse. We got talking about what I did for a living, and she just started to gush about how she doesn't like the church she grew up in, and is getting married but doesn't want to get married there, and how she thinks churches need to evolve with the times. And so I said, in my not so subtle way, "Have you heard about the United Church of Christ?" I then proceeded to tell her that we're the first Christian church to ordain an African American, woman, and gay and lesbian pastor, and that we're the only Christian church to have affirmed gay marriage, etc.—you know, the basic UCC stump speech. She then said, "Really, I didn't know a church like that existed!" So, come to find out, she's now going to be making a phone call to her local UCC church (the one where Kevin Goldenbogen did his student ministry) to see about getting married there. Who knows, maybe someday she'll become a member. See? It's as easy as that!

And second, since things have settled down a bit, people have started asking me how this whole ordeal has sat with me, from a faith perspective. In other words, am I mad at God for my son having had to go through all this? Well, if you were in worship to hear my sermon just before Jacob's surgery, or if you read it subsequently, then you've heard me speak to this (as an aside, if you'd like to read this, but haven't, just email me and I'll be happy to send it to you). To this question my response has always been, I'm not mad at God for this, because I don't believe that God causes people to have certain problems or go through particular difficulties in life. Rather, I believe that God is there to walk with us, and support us, through whatever may come our way. As such, I believe that Jacob's surgeries and Down syndrome are not a problem to lament, but rather a wonderful opportunity through which God will work to teach us all some important life lessons. That's not to say it's going to be an easy road, but I do believe that it is one that's ripe with possibility—in fact, it already has been. I think we are all very *different people than we were before Jacob was born, some 8 months ago. And this is only the beginning.*

Anyway, thank you for indulging me, once again, as I share my ponderings with you. I knew if I didn't share them now, then there might not be another opportunity to. So with that, I'm going to close the Chapter on Jacob's surgery. From here on out we'll try and update the page every so often—although much less frequently—just to keep you up to date with what's happening. Should Jacob end up back in the hospital (which we sincerely hope he won't), we will use this page to keep people posted again. But for now we hope that this will simply be a chance to update you on the positive progress that Jacob is making.

So even though the Revolution were painfully knocked out of the playoffs last night (which mercifully Jacob's tender heart didn't have to witness), it is a happy, happy day. Words cannot begin to say how much we have appreciated your words and your support—through this CarePage and through the many other ways you have reached out to us. This page started as a simple means of information dissemination, but quickly became a cathartic tool for me to process what was going on, and then evolved into so much more. It was a tremendous comfort and blessing to have you along on this journey with us—we are sincerely, sincerely indebted to you all for walking this sacred journey with us. We would not have made it without you.

With that I will give you one more clue to November 5th's post... if this doesn't give it to you, it'll remain a mystery for all time: "The beginning of each new thought adds up to something to celebrate." Good luck. And thank you, once again, for the bottom of our hearts. Kristen, Noah, Jacob and I love you all very much. Until next time...

Aren't you angry at God? (I guess we should finally entertain Eliphaz, Bildad, and Zophar's questions from the book of Job. You'll notice I never address Elihu. I never understood how he made it into the book anyway—someone's later addition probably. So I usually just pretend he's not there. Anyway....) I've heard the "angry at God" question from people before, and no doubt others struggling through a very Jobian stage in life have heard similar: Aren't you angry at God for what has happened to you? My answer is always the same: No. Even if I believed that God caused Jacob to be born with Down syndrome (which I don't, as I have said before), I still wouldn't be angry. I wouldn't be angry because I think that, sometimes, it's the toughest things in life that offer us the greatest blessings. As a pastor, I knew that in theory, and would say as much to those I was offering pastoral care to. Now I know it in reality, and can emphatically say the very same thing. I know other people have other reactions, but I honestly wasn't mad at God when I learned the reality of who Jacob was born to be. I didn't even ask why. I guess I just knew, deep down, that someday I would see that Jacob's birth was an incredible blessing. I just wasn't prepared for how many blessings would come my way. And so while I may sometimes wonder a little more earnestly about what God is up to, I can't see myself ever getting mad that Jacob was born with Down syndrome.

That's not to say that God can't handle our anger, or that it is a sign of our lack of faith if we do get angry—far from it. If something bad happens to us, then we have every right to rail against God. Children abused by their parents. Millions dying in a genocide. Famine sweeping across Africa. Elementary school students gunned down. A bombing at the hallowed ground of that blue and gold painted stripe on Boylston Street in Boston. That'll evoke my anger. That'll make me ask why God isn't calling more people to action to help (and also why more people aren't listening!). And in my anger I'd have good company. Ever read the Psalms? They're full of people taking some serious issue with how the Divine is running the world. The prophets? They're full of anger too. Even Jesus has a few choice words for God the night before he died: "Get rid of this cup, please!" And you know, God was big enough to handle those complaints, so God is big enough to handle ours as well. I just never felt that Jacob's Down syndrome was complaint worthy; which is odd because I can honestly say that I had little contact with the Down syndrome community prior to Jacob's birth. I didn't know a thing about the associated medical conditions, the day-to-day challenges of living, and the increased demands that such a child places on families. So, perhaps, you could say I was too ignorant to be mad. But in this case ignorance turned out to be incredible bliss.

It's not too much to say that my *entire* world view has changed. And I mean that. I see the world entirely different than I did before Jacob was born. I understand that every family has its challenges—some seen and some unseen. I now see that nearly everything I do—from working to shopping to running—can be an opportunity to help those who are struggling. And I try to grasp those opportunities. I have always been a "glass is half full" kind of guy, but I now see the world as a cup that has the possibility to brim over at every moment. And I'm doing my best to make that happen—to fill it with all I do and say. It's a view and a way of life that has impacted my friendships, my family, my relationships, and my job—all, I have to say, in a positive way.

Coming home and seeing my house, my family, and my church in a new way was just one example. Blessed, I'd have to say, doesn't quite capture it. But neither does angry.

NOVEMBER 14, 2008

There's no place like home!

So it's been a week since Jacob was released from the hospital. In many ways it seems like much longer than that. It has been so good to have everybody home together. We're starting to settle into a routine once again, and Noah has been just thrilled to be able to play with his Thomas and Friends train set all the time!

Jacob is doing well. I was met by the "oxygen people" as I call them, when I arrived home with Jacob last Friday. They brought us tons of oxygen. (Enough to cause some havoc, my doctoral classmates tell me, but I would never do anything like that!) Jacob is on oxygen 24 hours a day, but it is a very low dose. We just got a little machine to be able to measure his oxygen saturation today. He continues to run in the mid to upper 80s—which is pretty good. We don't know just when he'll lose the oxygen completely, but it's really not a big deal. We have a long oxygen cord, so we can carry Jacob around the house without too much trouble. The biggest issue is just trying not to trip over the cord! When Jacob went to the cardiologist today, they measured his saturation in the upper 80s even without oxygen on. So it seems like he's headed in the right direction. The issue remains keeping his oxygen up in the evenings, mostly.

At his cardiology appointment in Dover, the doctor told us that she was "amazed" at the repair they did on Jacob. She can't believe they were able to do what they did, and she said it looks fantastic. He looked much better than she thought he would, she told us the other day, so that is a very good sign. In addition to these very routine cardiology visits, Jacob also has a visiting nurse coming in a few times a week, a nutritionist coming in regularly, and he's being followed by his pediatrician. He's a well-cared-for-boy, for sure!

Jacob is on tons of medicine. We're weaning him off of a couple of painkillers (which is loads of fun), and he continues to be on: Lasix (to remove fluid around the heart)—he'll come off

this sometime in the not-too-distant future; Viagra (to reduce
the pressure in his lungs... incidentally, I learned that Viagra
was actually created for pulmonary hypertension, it only became
"popular" when they noticed the interesting side effect it had on
men... hmm...)–Jacob will be on that throughout the winter, just
so they can keep his lungs strong; he's on Albuterol and Pulmicort
(both are to help with his breathing)– he continues to sound
raspy, but he doesn't have a cold, just some "stuff" in his nose and
throat; and he's on Zantac, to keep his belly happy. So as you can
see, Kristen and I are earning our degrees with a crash course in
pharmacology.

As far as feeding goes, Jacob has his good days and bad.
They still have him on high-calorie formula (the same he was on to
beef him up pre-surgery), but we think he'll come off that soon. He
seems to get full pretty easy, plus the fact that he's weighing in at a
little over 15 pounds. Kristen has been calling him our 15- pound
butterball turkey, but you'd never hear such a comment from me :)
The food and weaning him off the painkillers have affected his sleep
some, but we're confident (or at least very hopeful!) that he'll get
back to sleeping through the night in no time.

Jacob doesn't appear to have regressed in terms of his social
interactions. He smiles, laughs, grabs at things, and makes noises at
us just like before. And he still loves to roll over whenever he gets the
chance. As I type this, he's sitting on the other couch, cooing away,
and grabbing at his tag blanket. Have I mentioned how nice it is to
be back home again?

So I think that's about all. Jacob has been "laying low" for a
while, and will continue to, for some time. He's still in a very fragile
state. Were he to come down with a cold, it could easily develop into
pneumonia, and we'd be right back in Children's. We think it's an
amazing hospital, but we're not in a hurry to go back as patients
any time soon!

Again, we thank you for your continued love, prayers, and
support. It has been great to see many of you again, and I look
forward to catching up with those of you I haven't seen yet very
soon! Check out the pictures as we've added a couple from home,
and we promise to keep you updated with semi-regular frequency
(i.e., when we think of it!). Anyway, since Jacob is doing raspberries
beside me, I guess that means it's time to go. Until next time...

Different hopes and different dreams. Upon leaving the hospital different hopes and different dreams was the new norm for us.

With tons of medicines, an oxygen cord trailing around the house, and in-home therapies starting, normal did take on a whole new meaning. Yet in some ways, life was very much the same. We still wanted the same thing for Jacob that we wanted for Noah and that we would wish for all people: that they can grow up to the best of their abilities and fulfill their potential. That's certainly what we were hoping would happen with Jacob.

And it has. As I'm writing this, Jacob is just over five years old and preparing for kindergarten. It took him a long time to sit up on his own (around fourteen months), and to walk (not until he was almost three). We're still waiting for him to talk, (save for a few babbles like "dada," "mama," "book," "Elmo," "Ah" (for Noah), "cup," "please," to name a few). He still struggles to eat on his own, and we won't even get into potty training for a while (nor Jacob's love for pulling the toilet paper off the roll!)—but he's getting there. He's hitting every developmental milestone we had hoped he would, just in his own time. And that's the thing we've learned about Jacob. When he puts his mind to it he can do whatever he wants to do. He's smart, but boy is he stubborn! It's a journey of waiting until he's ready, and then helping to guide him toward those milestones in any way we can. Kristen, Noah, and I—along with the rest of our family—relish that opportunity. The new norm.

Just today I saw him make the sign language sign for "Dada" on his forehead while we were riding in the car. I saw him shake his booty to an *Imagination Movers* song on television (by far his favorite show), and I have delighted in his interest in curling up on my lap with a good book signing "more book please" (after which time he goes to Kristen's lap, Noah's lap, and the laps of anyone else in the room to hear the same story again!). It's the new normal in our lives, and we can't imagine what any other normal would be like.

And we're certainly glad we don't have to.

DECEMBER 1, 2008

Happy Thanksgiving!

Ok, so maybe we're a few days late, but we wanted to wish you all a very Happy Thanksgiving. As you know, we have much to be grateful for this year, and we hope you were all able to give thanks with your loved ones this past week. And while we've got you here, I suppose we'll give you a Jacob update too :).

Things are going well. In addition to the nutritionist working with him, Jacob has a visiting nurse coming by three times a week to check breathing, weight, etc. This morning she tested him for the first time without his oxygen on. Without he was running in the low to mid-80s, which suggests that he might need to stay on a little longer. She will continue to test him each time she comes back, just to see how he's progressing. They're also working to get us a machine to measure his oxygen level by ourselves (actually he has one, but it's made for adults, so it doesn't work too well—we're hoping they might get an infant size to us soon!). This machine will enable us to get reads when he eats, sleeps, etc., so they can begin to decide when to take off his oxygen. They haven't ruled out keeping him on it all winter—just to lend him a hand—but it's too early to make that call now. For now we continue to juggle oxygen tanks when we venture outdoors, try not to break our necks on the 25-foot cord that's been winding its way around our house, and we make sure that we don't light any candles—oxygen and matches… not such a good mix!

Jacob continues to be on a lot of medicine. While the pain killers are finally gone (yeah!) he's still on a bunch of others— Zantac, Lasix, Sildenafil (Viagra), and Albuterol and Pulmicort nebulizers. While it's a lot to juggle, we've gotten into the rhythm of his days now. Those of you who have had infants know what it's like to live your life in 3-hour shifts (can I get to the store before his next feed…), we're living in between feeds and meds! So it does get complicated from time to time, but we're managing.

Unfortunately, because this is cold and flu season, Jacob isn't venturing out too far. Should he get sick, it can very easily develop into pneumonia, and then we'd find ourselves back in Chateau-Children's—not the place we want to be if we can help it! So, we call ahead if we're going to a relative's house to make sure no-one is sick before we go, and we've been trying to keep him out of public places as much as possible. This, I know, has been hard on our church family because everyone wants to see him, but it's going to be just a little longer before we bring him around such a large group of people. For now, you'll just have to enjoy Noah and the pictures of Jacob on the CarePage here (which reminds me, check out the new ones!).

Let's see, what else can I tell you… Early Intervention will be in to see Jacob in a couple of weeks. They will assess what therapies he will be getting in the months and years ahead. Other than that, things are great. Jacob has started to sleep through the night again (not every time, but we're getting there), and he's the happiest kid to be around. He gives you huge smiles that will make your heart melt, and can belly laugh so hard that he gets the whole room going with him. And Noah, of course, continues to be the wonderful big brother that he is—singing and trying to keep Jacob happy whenever he's cranky.

So, as always, thanks for your love, prayers, and support. Kristen's mother has decided that Jacob's hair looks better combed down over his forehead instead of pushed off to the side (the Donald Trump comb-over look). I think the "new look" makes him look like one of the Beatles. We'll post soon and let you decide. Until then, just imagine Jacob singing, "We love you, yeah, yeah, yeah…" Until next time…

Premarital counseling. I think that's the place in my ministry where Jacob's journey has come the most into play. Interesting, to think about—and not what I expected to be the case—but it's the truth. For better or for worse, most families in the church aren't dealing with difficult prenatal diagnoses, but rather are dealing with the just-as-tumultuous road of raising and rearing typically developing children.

So it's when starry-eyed, ready for marriage couples come into my office that I make sure that Jacob comes up in conversation. "What would you do," I ask, "if you found out that it was possible that your child had a condition like Down syndrome? Would you have the doctors perform an amniocentesis, even though it carries the risk of miscarriage (yes, my bias is showing)? Would you choose to abort the pregnancy? Would you give the baby up for adoption? And what if you found out that the baby had such a differing ability *after* he or she was born, would that change things?" Doing my best Muhammad Ali impersonation, the questions come in a barrage of verbal jabs.

Mostly they catch the couple off guard. I can almost see it in their eyes: "Why are we talking about this?" they wonder, as they are walking toward the happiest day of their lives, but seldom say out loud. Most couples say that this is something that they haven't had a chance to talk much about, and promise that they will. Others say that they have had these conversations, and I applaud them for their willingness to talk about such difficult subjects. Then I confess to them (which normally I haven't already) that our son Jacob has Down syndrome, and that Kristen and I *didn't* have a lot of these conversations prior to his birth. Fortunately Kristen and I were on the same page (no amniocentesis and a willingness to love, and keep, our baby—whoever he or she was born to be), but the results could have been disastrous. If we had wanted two different things, there's no telling what might have transpired between us.

And this uncertainty surrounding raising a child with Down syndrome is incredibly common. Although a quick Internet search will reveal a variety of different numbers, in a 2009 article ABC News reports that as many as 92 percent of women who receive a Down syndrome diagnosis choose to have an abortion. [27] This, even though a series of surveys in 2011 conducted by Dr. Brian Skotko while then working at Boston Children's Hospital revealed that: 79 percent of parents reported that their outlook on life was more positive because of their child with Down syndrome; 97 percent of siblings age twelve and older express pride about their brother or sister with Down syndrome, and 88 percent said they were better people because of their sibling; 99 percent of people with Down syndrome are happy with their lives, 97 percent like who they are, and 96 percent like how they look.[28] Is it any wonder, then, that since giving children with Down syndrome up for adoption remains a common occurrence, there are groups that have emerged for which the sole purpose is to help families adopt children *with* Down syndrome?

Now I'm not one to stand in the way of a woman's choice to have an abortion. Neither my personal faith convictions nor personal social stances compel me to do that. I do not believe that my faith or the government should regulate a woman's body. Abortion is a personal choice that is, sometimes, the best option—especially in cases of rape, incest, and other difficult circumstances. Had we known that Jacob had Down syndrome prior to his birth (interestingly, the doctors suggested that even though Jacob had a known heart defect the signs seemed to point to him *not* having Down syndrome), we wouldn't have aborted. It just wasn't a choice we were going to make. Had we found out that there was something severely wrong with our child that would endanger his or Kristen's health, we might have made a different choice, but that wasn't the case. When we made our marriage vows we promised to love each other no matter what, and in our book that meant even if our child was going to have some extra challenges in life.

So this is the conversation that I provoke in premarital counseling. The couples may leave wondering why we spent so much time on this and perhaps they'll argue a little about their answers to the questions, but I think it's only for their benefit in the long run. Having a child with differing abilities can be frustrating and challenging. If a couple is expecting to have a typically developing child and then find out that that's not the case, and if they haven't had any conversation about it, it can be an incredibly trying period of time while they try to figure out where they are in the wilderness. I guess I just want them to make sure that they have talked it through and weighed their options, before deciding to remove an incredible blessing that's about to come into their lives. But then, that's just me.

Yet it's possible that those blessings will be fewer and further between. At the time of the publication of this book, a new test was being developed that will help determine whether there are "problems" with a fetus, without the invasiveness and risks that an amniocentesis carries with it. This blood test—with reportedly no false-negatives in clinical testing—will effectively allow mothers to determine whether or not their baby is 100 percent healthy. Although it is suggested that this blood test will only be used for mothers who fall into the "high-risk" category, it's not a stretch to say that is the top of a very slippery slope. How long will it be before every mother gets such a test? How long will it be before aborting a fetus with Down syndrome is the norm (if it's not already)? And does this mean we're moving into the realm of designer babies—where eye color, hair color, even intelligence can be ascertained, and if not acceptable, aborted before it's "too late"?

As I said, I'm not one to stand in the way of a woman getting an abortion. That's an intimate, personal decision that is not without its own pains. But it saddens me to think that, if this becomes the norm, Jacob could be among the last in our society to be born with Down syndrome. What will life be like for him when he is older and his journey on this earth is nearing an end? Will acceptance begin to wane, as people have fewer interactions with people with Down syndrome? Will the medical community know how to treat people with Down syndrome (akin to the way many doctors no longer know how to treat postpolio patients since the eradication of the disease)? And most importantly, will this deprive the world of the unique joys that the Down syndrome community brings to the world?

In other memoirs that I have read by parents of children with Down syndrome, the question is invariably raised: Would you take away your child's Down syndrome if you were able to? My answer has always been: No. Without Down syndrome, Jacob is not Jacob. Without Down syndrome, I am not who I am. Without Down syndrome, Jacob would not have blessed us as richly as he has. Without Down syndrome, Jacob would not bless the world as richly as I believe he will.

Without Down syndrome, the world will be sadder place. And that's not a world I'm eager to live in.

DECEMBER 18, 2008

Merry Christmas!

Well like everyone else in these parts, we're still recovering from quite a weekend. We went 65 hours without power (much less than some of you) and so we had to take off for Massachusetts. With no heat source and Jacob needing electricity for his nebulizer treatments, we didn't have much of a choice. So it was off to Mimi and Grampy's again (a nice place to be, but where we're quickly wearing out our welcome, I think!) So it is good to be back home, and getting life back to normal again (gee, haven't I said that on this page before?) Anyway...

Jacob is doing really well. He went to his cardiologist on Tuesday, and she said he's looking the best she has ever seen him. Cardiac-wise he's still healing inside, but she can't get over how good the repair looks. He's still on oxygen (running in the 88-90% range without it on), so until he can stay in the 90s consistently, he'll need to keep wearing it. They just don't want his heart to have to work too hard, while it's still healing. In the next two weeks he'll be completely off his Lasix, which will bring him down to just three meds—Albuterol (through a nebulizer for his breathing), Zantac, and Sildenafil (Viagra)... which reminds me...

Our insurance company decided that they didn't want to pay for Jacob's Viagra. Since Viagra isn't an approved med by the company, they decided we could foot the bill on our own. So just go and get the generic, you're thinking, right? Not so fast! Viagra is normally in pill form. Jacob needs it in liquid form. So we have to go to a special pharmacy to get it mixed up. Hence, no generic. This means we were set to foot the bill for some $150 a month for this one med. Not what we wanted to hear. So our cardiologist called up the insurance company, assured them that our nine month old was not using the medicine to, shall we say, improve his performance, *and they finally agreed to pay. Which is nice, given that Jacob pretty much needs this medicine to stay alive! So now we get to fight for a refund for the last two months—but at least they'll be paying from this time forward!*

Ok, back to Jacob... Early intervention had to cancel on us. Jacob was supposed to be evaluated earlier this week, but they were under the weather. So he'll see them after the first of the year. And he continues to see his visiting nurse, two times per week.

So that's about all. Jacob is once again the smiley, happy boy that we knew before his surgery. He is sleeping through the night again, thankfully, and Noah's getting him (or at least trying to get him) pumped for Christmas. (It isn't working too well, but Noah has enough excitement for both of them!) Jacob's smiling, laughing, rolling over, and in love with looking at his hands—go figure!

That's about all. Go and check out the pictures we added, sans oxygen for the annual Christmas card shoot. And while we're talking Christmas, there are only six shopping days left (gasp!). So if you're struggling to give a gift, why not give that special someone a truly unique gift this year—a donation to a charity of your choice. Mine for this year is Children's Hospital. After all they have done for Jacob, I can't think of a better gift to receive than for Children's to receive some money to assist the good work they do. So I hope you'll consider doing something similar this year for those you love the most—be it to Children's Hospital or to the charity that touches your heart the most. With that, let me wish you all a very Merry Christmas and a Happy New Year! We thank you for the continued prayers, and we are certainly counting our blessings this Christmas season. See you in 2009! Until next time...

I believe our faith compels us to make a difference in this world, and the insurance companies are one place that could use a lot of faithful attention. Unlike our elevator acquaintances turned friends—who have had an incredibly horrendous battle with their insurance company—Jacob's struggles were minimal—but a challenge nonetheless. We made joke after joke about Jacob being on Viagra in our CarePage posts, but the fact of the matter is, this ended up being a huge challenge for us. Because of the "popular" use for this pulmonary hypertension drug, we nearly had to shell out more money (in addition to the thousands our insurance company already wasn't paying) to ensure that Jacob had the medication he needed to *live*. That's right, we weren't talking about elective medicine that would enable Jacob to "perform" well on a Friday night; this was medicine that he needed to stay alive. But the insurance company didn't want to hear that. Thankfully Kristen knew how to wade through those muddy waters, from her work at the pediatrician's office, so she was able to get things rectified—but it's a problem we shouldn't have been having.

Let's look at this objectively. I keep saying that having a child with differing abilities is a blessing. And it is. But it's also a challenge. Jacob was on oxygen. He was still on three different medications. He was receiving two to three in-home early intervention services per week. He had cardiology appointments. He had a few extra checkups at his pediatrician's office. All this in addition to the regular challenges that come with raising a newborn. Wouldn't it have been nice if the insurance companies didn't add to that list of challenges? Call me a socialist if you want, but I think it's a matter of faith that the insurance companies need to stop turning such a profit, while families struggle to procure the medicines and services that their children need to live.

A snap shot of life with a child of differing abilities. Jacob's third Christmas rolled around as he was nearing his third birthday. Noah, at five years old, was all gung-ho for Santa Claus to arrive. Mercifully Noah is not one of those "I want, I want, I want" children, but he was still excited to see what bounty awaited him on Christmas morning. Jacob? Not so much. We arrived downstairs to open our presents and began with the ones Santa had left unwrapped in front of the tree. Jacob perused his (a door that opens and closes, plays music, and lights up) for a few minutes. Then, as we were about two presents into our Christmas extravaganza, Jacob crawled into the living room, hopped up into the chair he has in front of the television, and made it known that he was ready to have breakfast and watch the *Imagination Movers*.

An incredulous Noah watched him with his jaw on the floor. "How could Jacob turn away from all these presents?" I could almost hear him wondering. "And does this mean that I don't get to open any more of mine?" I have to say that Noah was good about this hitch in plans. We proceeded to open up presents—just the three of us—while Jacob watched his show, and crawled into the other room to be with us from time to time. Christmas, to Jacob, was like any other day of the week, and he was bound and determined to stick to his favored routine.

Some will say that's because children like Jacob don't understand celebrations like Christmas. Granted he was just two-and-a-half, but still many typically developing children of that age have a sense of what Christmas is all about (presents, right?). For Jacob that wasn't yet the case. Eventually he will understand what Christmas is about—at some level—and perhaps even enjoy breaking his routine for that one morning, but he wasn't there yet.

But the fact of the matter is, Jacob is a child, and will grow up to be an adult, with differing cognitive abilities. This has given rise to the question: What do people need to "understand" about their faith in order to participate in religion and eventually be saved? An interesting pondering that deserves some attention.

But let me first start by saying that I don't care about salvation. Yes, you heard that right, I really don't care about salvation. While I know there are church folk out there screaming heresy at me, it's true—I don't really spend a lot of time worrying about salvation. I believe that we all stand witness to God's love in a new and amazing way when this life comes to an end—in a way that we can't even begin to fathom—but that's not a reward to be earned. Rather, the gift of salvation is given freely by God's grace to all of God's children. So yes, that makes me a universalist. I do not believe that God saves some and damns some to eternal punishment in hell. Rather I think that we are all welcomed into God's loving arms of grace and mercy when this life comes to an end.

Now I know someone is going to ask if I *really mean* that God's arms are opened to *everyone* at the end of their earthly journeys. My answer to that is yes. For I believe that God's love holds a transformative power that is bigger and more powerful than any of us can understand. Which is to say that if God desires all of us to be saved (which I believe God does), then I think God gets what God wants—either during this life, or after. To say otherwise would be to suggest that humanity has more power than God—for if God wants us to be saved and some are not saved, doesn't that mean that humanity is more powerful than God? I don't buy it. I believe God has the power to save all people, and that God *does* save all people. How it happens is not for me to figure out. That's why I don't worry about salvation. I live my life in response to this gracious gift that God has given to us, and I choose to believe that we will all experience salvation—even, and especially, those with differing abilities.

Yet not all are so persuaded. For the question has been asked: "With regard to people with intellectual disabilities…how does God's saving grace intersect with their inability to respond, at least in any discernable manner, to the call of the gospel?"[29] In other words, if Jacob never really comes to understand what Christmas is all about, does that exclude him from being saved? This is a question asked by those who believe that salvation is something to be achieved, to be earned, to be accepted (so long as you profess Jesus Christ as your Lord and Savior, they will, of course, add).

And while I think that a thinking faith is something to be applauded, I do not believe that a well-articulated theology is a prerequisite for receiving God's love and grace when this life comes to an end. Otherwise that would mean that all infants and some children, the elderly with dementia and Alzheimer's disease, along with people of differing intellectual abilities would be excluded from that love. Not in my book. Not with my God.

And while we're at it, let's also move away from this notion that such people with differing abilities need to be "fixed" or "healed" by God. To suggest that God needs to "heal" those who are differently abled is to perpetuate the notion that they are less than whole in God's eyes. There is no need for fixing anyone or anything made in the image of God. And that extends to the afterlife as well. When we stand fully enveloped by the love of God when this life ends (which I do not believe is an embodied existence anyway), there will be no need of fixing there. God will welcome all of us—abled or differently abled—just as the persons we were created to be.

And those are persons in the image of God—a God who, in the form of the impaired Jesus Christ, as Nancy Eiesland was earlier quoted as suggesting, is, in God's own way, disabled. Thus, if God is disabled, it should stand to reason that those of differing abilities do not need to be fixed or healed. They are whole just the way they are. As Webb-Mitchell suggests: "Nowhere in Scripture is a person praised or rejected for physical, mental, or emotional abilities or limitations. God looks instead upon the heart, which is often used as a synonym for a person's character."[30] They are loved, cherished, welcomed, and saved as they are—as the imperfect children of God that they were created to be, just like the rest of us.

As author Frederick Buechner puts it: "When it comes to the forgiving and transforming love of God, one wonders if the six-week-old screecher [you know that child, you've heard him in church] knows all that much less than the Archbishop of Canterbury."[31] We can impress our friends all we want by spouting off the fanciest theological terms we know—pericope, eschatology, and transubstantiation, oh my!—but in the end, faith is, and always will be, a mystery.

So let's not worry about salvation—especially for those of differing abilities. Let's focus our time and attention, as people of faith, on making this world a better place.

Perhaps we can start with health care?

JANUARY 5, 2009

Happy New Year!

Well, it's hard to believe that 2009 has arrived already. Needless to say, 2008 was a trying year for us—not to mention the world—so we're ready to turn the page and start afresh (and inaugurate a new President in 15 days, but who's counting)! (It's also shocking that in just over two months, we'll be celebrating Jacob's birthday... wow, how did that happen... but anyway.)

The real reason for my update is because Child Development Services, the ones responsible for Early Intervention, arrived today. They did an evaluation of where Jacob stands on a number of different skills and abilities—and given his Down syndrome and his heart surgeries, he did very well. The "normal" range for these tests, they say, is about 85–100. In Self-Help skills Jacob scored a 64. This, they attribute in large part, to the diet Jacob has been on. Once he starts eating more food and less formula (something the nutritionist will be working with him on this coming Thursday), his score here should shoot up. But given that he's only on formula and oatmeal now (due in large part to them wanting to maximize his caloric intake while preparing and recovering from surgery), his number is a little low here.

In gross motor skills Jacob scored a 67. This wasn't a surprise either. Kids with Down syndrome are known to have low muscle tone, and that is true for Jacob. He can sit up with some help, but has no ability to do that on his own yet. His legs have no strength to hold himself up (even when you hold him under his arms), and while he can roll over from his back to his stomach with ease, he's unable to get from his stomach onto his back again. So this will be an area to focus on.

In communication Jacob scored an 84, and in social skills he scored somewhere between 90–92. This should come as no surprise to any of you who have spent time with Jacob. Like his older brother, he LOVES to talk and make noise. In fact, the other night Kristen and I were trying to watch something on television and couldn't because Jacob was making so much noise! He's making lots of different sounds now (Da-Da-Da being one of his favorites, of course!), and he's still interacting and smiling up a storm. The best is to see his reaction when we say "Noah"—watching his smile and his eyes scanning around to find his brother is priceless.

So we were happy with where Jacob landed on the assessment. We knew that he would be behind in some areas, but were impressed that even in those areas, his numbers were pretty solid. The plan now is for Jacob to have 12 weeks (15 sessions) of occupational and physical therapy. They will work on fine motor and gross motor skills with him. Our big goal from this is to have Jacob sitting up, on his own, by the end. If he can do that, then we think he'll be able to play with more of his toys, thus offering him more stimulation. So that's the goal—we'll see how he does!

Let's see, what else is happening... the visiting nurse and cardiologist continue to say that he's healing well and looking/sounding the best they have ever seen him. His oxygen levels are still down a bit, so he's still wearing the oxygen and likely will be throughout the winter. We're also trying to keep him as sheltered from germs as possible (which is tough with a preschooler at home), because Jacob getting sick would not be a good thing. But every day he stays well is another day for him to get stronger to fight off anything that may come his way.

We have been able to wean some of his meds. He's still on the Sildenafil (Viagra), the Zantac, and the Albuterol/Pulmicort nebulizers. However, the Lasix is down to just one dose a day and will be gone in the next week. It may be just one less med, but that's a step in the right direction!

Other than that, Jacob is doing very well. From the outside you wouldn't know what he had been through inside. Save for the oxygen (which people seeing him for the first time still don't know how to react to), he looks like any other baby—see the new pictures for yourselves. And we feel he's progressing very well. He's working on his own time schedule, and whatever that is, we're fine with that.

And so as we welcome this New Year, I have to say that bidding adieu to 2008 is bittersweet. Personally, I have to say that it was the most trying year of my life. To think that we had Jacob in the hospital for roughly 2 months still astounds me. However, in that

*year we also received a tremendous blessing. While both of our kids
are blessings in their own right, Jacob just seems to be a little extra
special. He has already done things for our family, and caused me
to see the world in a way that I had not thought possible before. All
that in just nine months. I can't wait to see what he'll do for us when
he has a whole year to work with!*

Happy 2009! Until next time...

Before Jacob was born (well before), I had a feeling that he was going to be a she, and that she would grow up to be a minister, just like her father. I'm not sure why, but I have never had the feeling that Noah would be a minister (he still wants to be President of the United States, as he'll tell you, whether you ask or not. I just have yet to break it to him that in this "free" country you need to be a multimillionaire to reside at 1600 Pennsylvania Avenue....). Perhaps Noah is destined to be called by God to serve the church, who knows; I just always thought that my second child would be the one to follow in my footsteps. Guess I was wrong about that one, right?

I'm not so sure. In his short life, Jacob has already challenged our church to think about itself in a new way (Open and Affirming, communion, sign language applause, to name just a few). I can't help but wonder whether he has more in store. While I'm not sure that ordination would be within Jacob's abilities (though who really knows), I could see him functioning as a Deacon or perhaps even a licensed minister (a designation given in the United Church of Christ to a person who performs a specific ministry within a church setting) someday. Maybe that's just a Dad and minister dreaming, but it's certainly not outside the realm of possibility.

What makes the conversation about Jacob different than other conversations about ministering with differing abilities, however, is the fact that Jacob's differing abilities are of an intellectual, not a physical, nature. So while there have been many—and rightly so—pages dedicated to inclusivity with regards to ministers and clergy who ambulate differently and have other physical challenges, the same attention has not been paid to ministers with varying intellectual abilities. For example, what would it mean to have a minister serving communion who couldn't articulate a belief (or lack thereof) in transubstantiation? What about a pastor preaching a sermon during Holy Week without a thorough understanding of the various atonement theologies? What about a person offering pastoral care who has never read Martin Buber's *I and Thou*? We've talked about welcoming such individuals into the church and allowing them to participate in worship, but what about leading worship? We value a learned clergy. After all, we don academic robes on Sunday mornings because we believe, highly, in the value of a good education for those who lead our churches. Thus, can such a system of beliefs and ecclesial practice be reconciled with a theological understanding that would allow a person of differing intellectual abilities to serve in a leadership role in the church?

I believe it can; and as such I am reminded of Paul's words to the church in Rome: "Do not claim to be wiser than you are" (Romans 12:16). I think sometimes, in the church, we can get so wrapped up in our intellectual pursuits, theological understandings, and standardized seminary educations, that we forget that many of the people God called to service would not be considered, by today's standards, *learned*: fishermen, shepherds, and a timid young woman named Mary, to name a few. God didn't appear to be checking references, reviewing resumes, and clarifying credentials when God called them. And that's because I believe that God calls us to the ministries we are capable of performing. For some that many mean being an exegetically savvy, eloquently spoken preacher in a thousand-member church. For others it may mean navigating the high stress, heavily emotional hallways of hospital chaplaincy. And, still for others, it may mean being recognized for their dedication in visiting those who are unable to come to church on their own. God certainly looked beyond intellect when assembling the cast of characters that traveled with Jesus to do God's work. And if God could look past intellectual differences then, I think that we in the church can, and should, do the same.

Now it may well be that Jacob will never want to become a minister, or may not be called to become an ecclesiastically recognized minister in a church (I say this because, whether officially recognized by the church, or not, we are *all* called to be ministers). My point is simply to say: Why not? Why couldn't a person of differing abilities be recognized for the gifts they possess and utilize as they minister in Christ's name? I can't think of a single reason why, and it doesn't appear that the pages of our scriptures suggest one either. As such, any church that finds reason to object, I believe, needs to rethink their understanding of what it means to be a child of God. For I have yet to find a perfect minister out there, and something tells me that I'm not going to be able to find one.

Which makes Jacob, like all of us, perfect for the job.

FEBRUARY 10, 2009

11 Months Old!

Wow…amazing how time flies! Jacob is 11 months old today. Which means that it was just about a year ago that Kristen and I were beginning to realize the scope of what would lay ahead for us (fortunately we didn't know all the details, or we would never have made it!). What an 11 months it has been!

Jacob had an appointment with his cardiologist today. Things appear to be looking good. He is still having some mixing of blood in his heart (nonoxygenated and oxygenated), and the blood is still not flowing into the reconstructed right chamber as much as they would like. They tell us this will continue to correct itself over time. His body is still adjusting to the major repair that happened. So they said to give it time. He's beginning to "outgrow" the Sildenafil (Viagra) and Lasix he has been receiving. This is a good thing, as it will make it easier on his body when he stops taking them. But this won't happen until at least April. That's when Jacob goes to see the cardiologist again, and she doesn't want to change anything until then. So he'll remain on oxygen and all his meds for another two months at least.

Which reminds me…the Viagra crisis continues! The insurance company still doesn't want to pay for this med (which is very expensive), thinking that Jacob is using the medicine for reasons other than reducing his lung pressure. They just can't quite figure out that an 11-month-old might have an alternate use for Viagra! So they are still not paying for it, and they have actually asked the pharmacy to alter the documents so that it will look like Jacob is getting less than he actually is—which they would then pay for. Not only is that dangerous, but incredibly unethical! The pharmacy (which is a specialized one) has refused to doctor anything, which is great. But I keep thinking we ought to file a complaint with the insurance company for even asking to do such a thing. But I'm not sure that's going to help get them to pay for the medicine! So we'll wait and see on that one. And who said that the health care system doesn't need to be fixed...anyway...

An occupational therapist from Early Intervention will be coming next Tuesday to start therapy with Jacob. We're very excited about this. Now we'll get a chance to see where he's at and what areas he needs to work on. From what we see, muscle tone is definitely the biggie. He still has no ability to sit up on his own (although he can do it for a few seconds from time to time). He can roll over and pick his head up off the ground, but that's about all. Socially, though, he is very engaging. He smiles, laughs, imitates us, babbles with a bunch of different sounds, grabs for things, and even gave Noah a high-five the other day. So that is all wonderful to see. Not knowing how he was going to develop, we're very impressed with where he is, and hope that this is a sign of good things to come!

We are still being very careful with Jacob. We're starting to bring him to more events at the church and such, but you'll notice that we're not offering him to people to hold, and he's often in his car seat or front pack. This is because Jacob's immune system isn't 100%. He has gotten one cold already, and made it through, but we don't want to chance fate with him getting a second (which could easily develop into pneumonia). So if you see Jacob, by all means come over and say "hi", but do us a favor, wash your hands before touching him, and please try not to touch his hands—that's the way most germs are passed and we'd like to avoid it. Soon enough you'll be able to hold him; just have a little patience until the winter is over.

So what else... you'll see that there's a new template for Jacob's CarePage. That's a special treat offered to us by CarePages (I liked the jungle animals over the rubber ducky). I've added a couple of new pictures for you to look at. And I want to share a wonderful book I have been reading with you... it's "Expecting Adam" by Martha Beck. This is an autobiography of a woman who learns that she is carrying a child with Down syndrome while working on her doctorate at Harvard. The book goes back and forth between all the "intellectuals" telling her not to have the baby, and many stories of the joy Adam has brought to her family's life. Whether you're the parent of a Down syndrome child or not, I'd highly recommend it— it's poignant and quite funny. Also, I should mention that February 14th is Congenital Heart Defect awareness day—smartly chosen, I would say! So please say an extra prayer on Valentine's Day for all those who are dealing with Congenital Heart Defects and their families.

I guess that's all for now. Thanks so much for your continued thoughts and prayers—we can't begin to tell you how instrumental your support has been in getting us through these 11 months. We couldn't have done it without you, and will continue to lean on you in the future, for sure! Until next time...

When people want to talk about the church being made up of a diverse group of people, they often quote from 1 Corinthians 12: "The body is one and had many members...." You know the passage. It's a beautiful text, and oft quoted for good reason, as it reinforces the idea that *all people* have a place and a job in the church. Some are high-functioning hands and feet, eyes or ears, while others are the no less essential (but certainly less flashy) eyelashes and eyebrows, spleens, and toenails of the body of Christ. But just what does that body look like? Is it a six-foot-four, muscular football player? Is it an overweight student? Is it a frail, elderly woman? Yes, yes, and yes. The body of Christ looks like all those, and more. Theologian Amos Yong even suggests that the body of Christ could be "a child with Down syndrome" calling attention to Renaissance painter Andrea Mantegna, and her painting *Virgin and Child,* which portrays the baby Jesus as characteristically having Down syndrome, "with the facial phenotype, wide spacing between the first and second toes, size of the child's fingers."[32] So yes, the body of Christ even looks like Jacob. Or perhaps better put, Jacob looks like the body of Christ.

With this image in mind—and with our disability theology hats on—I wonder if it isn't time for the church to adopt a new image of the body of Christ? Instead of the 1 Corinthians text, which implies that the many and varied body parts are moving in synchronized precision with one another, working just as a body should, perhaps there is a different image we can adopt—one in which the body may not be working as "perfectly" as the letter to Corinth seems to portray.

What about a mother holding her child with Down syndrome close to her breast in a front pack? Now granted, this isn't a single body of Christ, these are *bodies* of Christ—but then, as Christians, we are intended to be relational creatures, are we not? So why not paint a picture of the church—the body of Christ—which shows two bodies in relation to each other?

For the image of mother and child suggests that to be the church bodies need to be close with one another, intimately connected. There is no such thing as a body existing on its own, for its own good. In this image we see the child with Down syndrome held close to his mother's breast in such a way that illustrates the love that we are called to show for each other, and for God—a love no better exemplified than in the love that a mother holds for her child. It's one member of the body of Christ supporting another member (i.e., wearing the front pack) who is having some challenges; and the child is positioned in such a way that other bodies can come forward to show their love of and affection for that same member. It's the church being best at what it could and can be: a church of relationships and service to one another.

If we're looking for a new image of the church, then that's what I want it to be: mother carrying child. Maybe it'll catch on. Maybe it'll prompt a Facebook movement to add the newly inspired *3 Corinthians* to our canon of scriptures. Ok, probably not. But it is a pretty good image.

A new image of the body of Christ—another way Jacob is challenging the church to think about itself in a new way.

MARCH 10, 2009

Happy Birthday Jacob!

One year ago today, at this very hour, I remember where I was—vividly. Kristen and I were waiting in Brigham and Women's Hospital. In fact, we'd been waiting all day...literally. We went into the Hospital for a routine appointment, only to find out that the amniotic fluid around "the baby" (we didn't know boy or girl then) was low. So our doctor asked, smiling, if we were in the mood to have a baby that day. She didn't like the idea of the baby staying in with such low fluid. So began the journey.

In order to take one variable out of the equation (since they knew "the baby" had some problems), they told Kristen she'd be having a C-section. First she had to fast. The delivery was scheduled for early afternoon. But we got bumped, and bumped, and bumped again. You see, people kept coming in with "emergencies," and so we were the lucky ones to keep getting pushed back. By this time we were both starving. Kristen couldn't eat and I wouldn't eat in front of her. (This, despite the nurse pleading with me because she didn't want me to pass out in the delivery room!) It wasn't until sometime after 10 p.m. that Jacob Ottley Gallagher breathed his first breath of Boston (ok, sterile hospital room) air. Weighing in at 4 pounds 9 ounces, Jacob was actually bigger than Noah when he was born, believe it or not.

The birth was nothing like you see on TV. There were probably 20 people in the room with us. As soon as he was born, he was rushed over to a table to be examined. No chance for Dad to cut the cord this time. In fact, Jacob was probably 2–3 minutes old before someone thought to come over and tell us that we had had a boy. It was then that I got to go over and start snapping some photos. Racing back and forth between Jacob and Kristen (so I could show her what he looked like on the back of the digital camera), our journey began.

After they decided that Jacob was in no immediate danger, Kristen stayed in the operating room and I followed Jacob upstairs to a holding room before he went into the Neonatal ICU. It was a quiet room. Three or four babies were there being monitored very closely. No balloons, no teddy bears, just wires and monitors (the introduction to what would occupy so much of our life for the next year). The first doctor looking at Jacob hinted that he had some signs of Down syndrome, but not all of them. They'd need to do some blood tests. The real concern was the heart. So Jacob got swiftly moved across the bridge to Children's Hospital where he could have an echocardiogram done and eventually go in for his first—unplanned—surgery to repair his aortic arch. The rest, from there, is history.

Can you tell I'm feeling a bit nostalgic today? I had an opportunity to reflect quite a bit while riding home from Bangor this afternoon. Not only was I thinking about March 10, 2008, but also about all that Jacob went through last year, and how far he has come. Just the other day Jacob rolled over from his stomach to his back for the first time. He's getting a little more steady sitting up (although he needs some help), and his upper body is getting very strong. He loves to sit on Daddy's lap and clap Daddy's hands together. And let me tell you, he's got quite a grip! The OT work he's doing will hopefully help all of this development.

From here things will get interesting. Supposedly he is outgrowing his medicine, so that is likely to change. He'll be reevaluated as to whether or not he needs the oxygen anymore next month, and on Thursday his nutritionist will be revamping his food schedule. He's been eating a lot of late, so we're guessing that more "real food" will be in order, but we will see.

All in all he's doing incredibly well, we think. His vocalization and social skills continue to amaze us. I've been doing a fair amount of reading on Down syndrome, and so I'm beginning to wrap my mind around what's to come—the fact that he may not walk until he's 2 or 3, may not talk until that same time, will have his teeth come in a different order than other kids, etc. It's not the journey we expected to take, but we're having a blast. As our long-term CarePage readers will appreciate—we are loving every tulip and windmill that Holland has to offer!

And so we are celebrating. We're celebrating this amazing first year that Jacob has been through. We're celebrating the many, many gifts he has given us and lessons he has already taught us. We're celebrating that while every child is special in his or her own right, we've been blessed to have an extra special one with us for what has been an amazing year. We'll have a party with family on Saturday, and the church is throwing Jacob (and Noah) a party toward the end of the month. I hope many of you will come to celebrate not just Jacob's birthday, but all those in our midst who, though they are differently abled, have so much to teach the rest of us. To paraphrase Jennifer Graf Groneberg, the author of "Roadmap to Holland," which I just finished reading—Jacob isn't the child we expected, but he's the child we needed. We're learning that more and more every day.

And so I'll leave it with more nostalgia than medical jargon today. It's Jacob's first birthday, and given that there were a few times in the last year when we weren't so sure he'd make it this far, it is a day to celebrate!

I've been choked up all the way home on my ride from Bangor today listening a song by Darius Rucker (the former lead singer of Hootie and the Blowfish) called "It Won't Be Like This For Long." He thinks about his young daughter's life and anticipates just how fast her life—even the hard times—will go by. That certainly rings true for our journey with Jacob, as I know it will for those of you who have raised children of your own. The song is worth a listen, but I definitely recommend having a few tissues nearby.

Thanks, as always, for the prayers, love, and support. They mean more to us than we can possibly say. We are indebted to you all. Until next time…

Although our journey is far from over, Jacob's first birthday felt kind of like the end of one chapter and the beginning of another. As my favorite poet T.S. Eliot wrote: "In my beginning is my end."[33] So as one chapter ends, another, necessarily, begins. Our lives are one big book of chapters opening and closing, and Jacob's first chapter (or first book, you might say), has come to a close. As much as we would love to keep him as that tiny, cuddly one-year-old who hadn't learned how to throw yet, we must turn the page. And in that ending is the beginning of a journey that we can't scarcely begin to imagine, and can't wait to take!

For Jacob's birthday party (nontraditional, of course, as he is only now just beginning to be okay with people singing "Happy Birthday"), Kristen came up with an equally nontraditional party favor for all of Jacob's cousins. In lieu of stickers and yo-yos, we gave each of the families a copy of the book: *My Friend Has Down Syndrome* by Jennifer Moore-Mallinos. It's a wonderful book that introduces children to Down syndrome and what living life with someone with Down syndrome might be like. When my sister-in-law Diana approached her son Patrick to talk about this book with him, his response was simply: "Oh it means that it'll take Jacob a little longer to do things? That's okay." My hope and prayer is that all of Jacob's future interactions are with people who are so understanding!

It is a response that gives me tremendous hope. It's a theme that has run throughout this entire book, and so that's the note I want to end on: hope. Our Christian faith is built on the foundation of hope—hope for salvation, hope of forgiveness, hope of experiencing the love of God—and that's a hope that extends to all of God's children of all different abilities. It's a hope that I held for my two children before they were born, and a hope that I now hold for Jacob in a slightly different way. A hope that his life will be marked by acceptance and understanding as we work to help him reach his best possible potential—a potential that I believe the church will play an integral role in helping him realize.

Nancy Eiesland has been quoted as saying: "My disability has taught me who I am and who God is."[34] While I am not perfect, I do not have the differing abilities that Jacob has, and yet I do believe that his coming into my life has taught me who I am and what kind of a minister God has called me to be. Before, I might have been focused on changing the world through extraordinary acts of oratory and perhaps even climbing the ecclesiastical ladder to pastor the biggest church I could; now I see my role as helping to bring hope to the hopeless, to the downtrodden, to the excluded, to the disenfranchised, to those of differing abilities. For in bringing such hope I find that my hope and faith in God is strengthened. And as a pastor, that's a high enough achievement for me.

As Amos Yong rightly points out in his book *Theology and Down Syndrome*: Living with disabilities shapes our lives, relationships, and identities in substantive rather than incidental ways."[35] As Jacob's journey has shown, mine have been shaped in ways that I can only summarize as the greatest blessing that God has ever given to me.

Clearly our wilderness wanderings are not over. There will be more Walmarts, more bowling alleys, more services of communion, possibly more surgeries, but hopefully no more head-sniffers. That's life in the wilderness. And that's where we will wander the rest of our days. Yet it's such wanderings that have made me the father, the pastor, and the person that I am today. Other paths would surely have made the journey easier, but slowing down to savor the journey that Jacob is on has continued to make all of our lives better. I wouldn't change a step if I could.

We now have eyes to see, and hearts to feel, the wilderness blessings that God is bestowing upon us every day—and knowing the way the wilderness works, I believe the best is yet to come.

POSTSCRIPT

A fter writing what I thought would be this book's final words, I shut down my computer, left my office (where I'd been hiding out looking for some quiet space to write), and walked in our back door. Stopping to put my computer bag on the floor in its usual place, I heard the familiar—and uneven—thump, thump, thump of Jacob's heavy stride on our wooden floor. Looking up I saw a confident, three-and-half-year-old Jacob walking—no, strutting, as we more aptly describe it—unencumbered by feeding tubes or oxygen cords, no scars visible to see—around the corner, toy in his left hand, his right hand waving vigorously, a gleam in his eyes, with an open-mouthed smile that went from ear to ear.

When he got to my feet, he raised his arms up high, fingers tugging at my belt. I reached down and picked him up, only to feel his arms wrap tightly around my neck—his toy-free hand patting my back in an embrace not unlike old friends would share.

It was then I realized that I was wrong. The best is not yet to come. The best is already here.

Until next time….

NOTES

1 Elizabeth A. Johnson, *She Who Is: The Mystery of God in Feminist Theological Discourse* (New York: Crossroad, 2000), 253.

2 Ibid., 267.

3 Jesse Rice, *The Church of Facebook,* (Colorado Springs: David C. Cook, 2009), 170.

4 Alister E. McGrath, *Christian Theology, An Introduction,* 3d ed. (Malden, Mass.: Blackwell, 2001), 253.

5 Ibid.

6 Nancy L. Eiesland, *The Disabled God* (Nashville: Abingdon Press, 1994), 100.

7 Ibid., 101.

8 Amos Yong, *Theology and Down Syndrome* (Waco, Texas: Baylor University Press, 2007), 175.

9 Eiesland, 116.

10 Thomas E. Reynolds, *Vulnerable Communion, A Theology of Disability and Hospitality* (Grand Rapids: Brazos Press, 2008), 207.

11 Brett Webb-Mitchell, *Dancing with Disabilities, Opening the Church to All God's Children* (Cleveland: United Church Press, 1996), 68.

12 Psalm 36:8.

13 Reprinted with permission. Copyright © 1987 by Emily Perl Kingsley. All rights reserved.

14 In this sermon I compared our journey with Jacob with the biblical story of Jacob wrestling with God in Genesis 32:22–31 and with the disciples' wilderness feelings in Matthew 14:13–21.

15 William H. Willimon, Pulpit Resource, Vol.36, No.3, Year A, July, August, September, 2008, (Inver Grove Heights, Minn.: Logos Productions, Inc., 2008), 24.

[16] Much of the following information is taken from the website of the National Down Syndrome Society: www.ndss.org.

[17] Webb-Mitchell, 51.

[18] Quinn G. Caldwell and Curtis J. Preston, eds., *The Unofficial Handbook of the United Church of Christ* (Cleveland: United Church Press, 2011), 34.

[19] As is so often the case with technology, between this post and the last one CarePages updated its servers to include titles with each entry. So the remaining entries will now include the titles they were given when composed.

[20] Marcus J. Borg, *The Heart of Christianity* (San Francisco: HarperCollins, 2003), 156.

[21] Abraham Joshua Heschel, *I Asked for Wonder* (New York: Crossroad, 2010), 49.

[22] Frederick Buechner, *Wishful Thinking, A Seeker's ABC* (San Francisco: HarperCollins, 1993), 76.

[23] Taken from the Open and Affirming Statement adopted by our congregation on May 15, 2011.

[24] It was written by Geoffrey Douglas.

[25] Harold C. Washington, "Fear," in *The New Interpreter's Dictionary of the Bible, D-H, Volume 2,* ed. Katharine Doob Sakenfeld, et al. (Nashville: Abingdon Press, 2007), 441.

[26] Christopher W. Perry, *The Church Mouse,* (Cleveland: Pilgrim Press, 2011), 39.

[27] Taken from http://abcnews.go.com/Health/w_ParentingResource/down-syndrome-births-drop-us-women-abort/story?id=8960803.

[28] Taken from http://www.msnbc.msn.com/id/44703812/ns/health-health_care/t/down-syndromes-rewards-touted-new-test-looms/#.ToTU_3ZeJYM.

[29] Yong, 232.

[30] Webb-Mitchell, 41.

[31] Ibid., 22.

[32] Yong, 175 and 176.

[33] T.S. Eliot, *Four Quartets, East Coker, I* (San Diego: Harcourt Brace & Company, 1971), 20.

[34] Yong, 268.

[35] Ibid., 269.